THE
LAVENDER
COMPANION

THE
LAVENDER
COMPANION

ENJOY *the* AROMA, FLAVOR, *and*
HEALTH BENEFITS *of This* CLASSIC HERB

TERRY BARLIN VESCI

with JESSICA DUNHAM

photographs by TOSCA RADIGONDA

Storey Publishing

The mission of Storey Publishing is to serve our customers by
publishing practical information that encourages
personal independence in harmony with the environment.

EDITED BY Carleen Madigan and Lisa H. Hiley
ART DIRECTION AND BOOK DESIGN BY
  Carolyn Eckert
TEXT PRODUCTION BY Jennifer Jepson Smith
PHOTO STYLING BY Ann P. Lewis
FOOD STYLING BY Terry Barlin Vesci
FOOD STYLING ASSISTANT Sabra Sanders

COVER AND INTERIOR PHOTOGRAPHY BY
  © Tosca Radigonda
ADDITIONAL PHOTOGRAPHY BY © Alexander
Zatschkovitsch/GAP Photos, 21 r.; © Andy Vesci,
14, 143 b.l. and t.r., 149, 156 l.m.; © Anne Gilbert
/Alamy Stock Photo, 25; Annie Spratt/Unsplash,
10; Bia Octavia/Unsplash, 20; © Botanic World
/Alamy Stock Photo, 138 r.; Carolyn Eckert © Storey
Publishing, 21 l.; (c) Chris Burrows/GAP Photos,
23 b.r.; © Dave Zubraski/GAP Photos, 23 b.l.; Despond
Lingard/Unsplash, 128; H. Zell/CC BY-SA 3.0/
Wikimedia Commons, 11 t.l.; © JS Sira/GAP Photos,
23 t.l., 138 l.; © Maddie Thornhill/GAP Photos, 130;
© Madeleine Steel/Shutterstock, 11 t.r.; Mars Vilaubi
© Storey Publishing, 26, 27 (all but 'Provence'), 40,
43 (bckg.), 52–58, 60–63, 70, 147 (bckg.); © Matt
Anker/GAP Photos, 23 t.r.; ©Peter Jordan_NE/Alamy
Stock Photo, 131; © PhanuwatNandee/iStock.com,
11 b.l.; Rebecca Niver/Unsplash, 129; © Wrangler-JT/
iStock.com, 11 b.r.

TEXT © 2024 BY Terry Barlin Vesci and Jessica Dunham

This publication is intended to provide educational
information for the reader on the covered subject.
It is not intended to take the place of personalized
medical counseling, diagnosis, and treatment from
a trained health professional.

The information in this book is true and complete
to the best of our knowledge. All recommendations are
made without guarantee on the part of the authors or
Storey Publishing. The authors and publisher disclaim any
liability in connection with the use of this information.

The publisher is not responsible for websites (or their
content) that are not owned by the publisher.

Storey books may be purchased in bulk for business,
educational, or promotional use. Special editions or
book excerpts can also be created to specification.
For details, please contact your local bookseller or the
Hachette Book Group Special Markets Department
at special.markets@hbgusa.com.

STOREY PUBLISHING
210 MASS MoCA Way
North Adams, MA 01247
storey.com

Storey Publishing is an imprint of Workman Publishing,
a division of Hachette Book Group, Inc., 1290 Avenue
of the Americas, New York, NY 10104. The Storey
Publishing name and logo are registered trademarks
of Hachette Book Group, Inc.

ISBNs: 978-1-63586-684-1 (hardcover);
978-1-63586-685-8 (ebook)

Printed in China through Asia Pacific Offset on paper
  from responsible sources
10 9 8 7 6 5 4 3 2 1

Library of Congress Cataloging-in-Publication Data
  on file

There are only two ways to live your life. One is as though nothing is a miracle. The other is as though everything is.

—ALBERT EINSTEIN

Farmers and gardeners live as though everything is a miracle. How could we not?

Dedicated to my husband, Rick, and our wonderful kids— where would I be without you?

CONTENTS

THE JOY OF LAVENDER

My love of cooking, preserving, and baking, and my passion for creating a warm and inviting home, started in 1977 with a still-cherished book, *Farm Journal's Freezing & Canning Cookbook*. It's filled with my handwritten notes—not only thoughts on my favorability rating of a recipe but also notes about my life at the time, like the otherwise beautiful fall day when my son Aj went off to college or the time my husband and I went on our first date. It's marked with little asides about cookies baked for friends and even tears over a favorite cake recipe I made for a beloved dog (yes, you read that right). All these things remind me of days gone by. The *Farm Journal's Freezing & Canning Cookbook* reads like my personal journal. As a lavender farmer and chef, I guess it's fitting that my diary makes its home in a cookbook.

The recipes in that book, and the way it connected cooking, preserving, making, and baking directly to hearth and home, inspired me. It gave me the dream of owning a farm one day and helped me imagine what that dream might look like. In 2015, that dream came true when my husband, Rick, and I bought a historical homestead in Pine, Arizona, boldly planted 5,500 lavender plants, and opened Pine Creek Lavender Farm.

At the farm, we operate a Lavender Cooking and Baking School. We also operate a popular farm store and an online retail shop that sells lavender products. Over the past few years, I've seen firsthand how lavender can change people's lives, whether it's lavender essential oil helping a young girl finally find sleep after years of stressful deprivation (as a last resort, her primary care physician sent her family to us) or helping home cooks and professional chefs alike discover the amazing variety in the tastes of lavender.

Our life now is farm life, with work dictated by the rising and setting of the sun and our habits ruled by the rhythms of the seasons. We are proud that we have created a legacy of land, water, history, and lavender farming that we can pass along to our kids and grandkids.

A while ago, Rick and I visited Amish Country, where I spied a beautiful and expensive cookbook. He gently pointed out that I already own over 200 cookbooks! But if you're like me, you know a cookbook is so much more than a collection of recipes. It's a tangible link to people and places, to memories of the fun trip we were having, to new ideas and tastes. I bought the book and now it's a new favorite—scribbled with notes, stained with butter and cream.

My heartfelt hope is that this book becomes that for you: a go-to resource and a journal of your love of food, new ideas, and home. Please scrawl notes in the margins. Bend down pages of recipes and projects you want to make. Share it with a friend and save it for your kids or grandchildren so they'll see what you loved, too.

If you do that, then I'll know this book was a success. However you choose to use it, let it serve as inspiration for all the ways you can bring the beauty, fragrance, and flavor of lavender into your home. And for goodness' sake, get in touch at pinelavenderfarm.com and tell me what you loved the best!

XO

Jerry

A FAVORITE HERB
through the ages

Lavender has long been a beloved herb, not only for its fragrant aroma but also because of its distinct flavor as a seasoning and its well-documented calming properties for stress, anxiety, and muscle tension. Today, the production of lavender, especially lavender essential oil, is a multibillion-dollar industry, clearly indicating its worldwide popularity as an ingredient in household and beauty products, as a plant in gardens and landscaping, and as a health aid in the latest medicinal applications. But its popularity dates back some 2,500 years.

Lavandula, a genus with nearly 50 species of flowering plants, is an evergreen shrub native to Mediterranean countries, such as Spain, France, Italy, and Greece. It grows in temperate climates and in places as diverse as the Middle East, England, and parts of North America (including Arizona!).

One of the most multifaceted of herbs, lavender has been grown for centuries all over the world and used in multiple ways. Supposedly it was in ancient Arabia that lavender was first farmed and distilled for its oils. Doctors in ancient Greece used lavender to relieve indigestion, headaches, and sore throats. English and French herbalists used lavender to aid sleep—much as we do today—by stuffing it into pillows. They also used it for headache relief.

Modern uses for lavender aren't so different. When commercial lavender production began in the 1940s, interest in the herb as a culinary ingredient and a key component in health and wellness became more widespread in North America. The Shakers were the first to grow lavender as a cash crop, creating herb farms to produce and sell medicinal lavender products. Now it's cultivated for commercial use primarily in Bulgaria, the United States, Canada, France, England, Japan, Italy, Australia, and New Zealand.

One of the most multifaceted of herbs, lavender has been grown for centuries all over the world and used in multiple ways.

Lavender and Wellness

The science on lavender and its health benefits is surprisingly abundant, especially compared to that of other plants. Clinical trials conducted by medical research facilities, such as the University of Maryland Medical Center, the University of Arizona Andrew Weil Center for Integrative Medicine, and the division of life sciences at Kagoshima University in Japan (among many others), indicate that lavender contains powerful antibacterial, antiviral, and antimicrobial properties.

Lavender contains polyphenols and flavonoids, plus aromatics and the anxiety-relieving components linalool and linalyl acetate. Like sage and rosemary, lavender also contains the terpenes cineole and camphor. These components work together to provide lavender's health-boosting power. Studies show that using the herb can help ease anxiety, induce sleep, relieve pain from headaches, soothe stomachaches, heal minor skin wounds, reduce stress, boost mood, and improve memory.

STOMACH SOOTHER

Lavender can treat many digestive concerns, such as nausea, bloating, intestinal gas, and loss of appetite. One study found lavender essential oil was more effective than ginger essential oil when inhaled as a remedy for nausea and vomiting. Another study suggested that chewing on a stalk of culinary lavender offers the same benefits.

Lavender can be used as a fresh or dried herb. It is also widely used as an essential oil. There are three principal ways to derive the unique health benefits of lavender.

TOPICAL, applying it to the skin for absorption

OLFACTORY, breathing it in to stimulate olfactory neurons

INGESTION, through foods or drinks containing lavender

Aromatherapy Began with Lavender

In the 1930s, chemist René-Maurice Gattefossé burned his hand. He treated the burn with lavender oil, and after witnessing how fast the burn cooled and the wound healed, he published a treatise on the medicinal use of essential oil and the possible therapies of aromatic plants, even coining the now-familiar term "aromatherapy."

French biochemist Marguerite Maury used Gattefossé's idea to develop an effective method of systematically applying essential oils to the skin, a practice known today as aromatherapy massage.

'GROSSO'

'ROYAL VELVET',
mint, lemon balm,
and rosemary

Lavender *in the* Kitchen

Along with other culinary herbs like mint, basil, sage, and rosemary, lavender is part of the mint family (Lamiaceae). The ancient Greeks and Romans cooked with it, enjoying its lightly sweet and floral fragrance in their dishes. Lavender is often used on its own as an ingredient or as one of several herbs in herbes de Provence.

Today, both home cooks and notable chefs find lavender to be a delicious and versatile ingredient. Its uses include adding flavor to ice cream, scones, breads, and cakes; making infused oils and honeys; seasoning salads and marinating meats; employing as a dry rub; and even mixing it into your favorite happy hour drinks.

Lavender *in the* Garden

Though lavender was likely planted as a beautiful addition to landscapes centuries ago, it came into prominence in the late 1800s. That's when Queen Victoria bestowed the title of Purveyor of Lavender Essence to the Queen on lavender distiller Sarah Sprules. Sprules became known worldwide for her lavender water, and her products became highly sought after as gifts for royalty, including royalty from other countries. As lavender's popularity grew in the English court, women all over England started growing the herb as an ornamental plant in their gardens.

Not only is lavender perfect for gardens—it looks gorgeous mixed in with other colorful plants and blooms—it's also ideal for containers or pots, flower beds, and farms. In fact, there are more than 700 farms in the United States registered with the United States Lavender Growers Association.

HEALTH BOOSTER

Lavender is a boon for overall health. The National Library of Medicine noted a study of 100 patients in the intensive care unit who had lavender essential oil massaged into their feet. Each patient showed signs of improved health, such as lowered blood pressure, heart rate, and respiratory rate and reduced pain.

Even better, lavender acts as a purple magnet for crucial pollinators such as bees, butterflies, and hummingbirds. Why crucial? Because according to the U.S. Department of Agriculture, three-fourths of the world's flowering plants and about 35 percent of the world's food crops depend on animal pollinators to reproduce. Put another way: That's one out of every three bites of food we eat.

So Many Ways to Use Lavender

In addition to its uses for cooking, mixology, and well-being, lavender is a favorite among crafters, artists, and DIY makers. Dried lavender lends an elegant touch to home décor such as culinary braids, table centerpieces, wreaths, home-crafted soaps and wax melts, and more. In a mist or spray, lavender has been found to help repel mosquitoes, flies, and rodents.

Lavender's scent infuses the home in sachets or candles. It enhances relaxation as an aromatherapeutic bath bomb or shower steamer. And fields of lavender in shades of lilac, violet, pink, royal purple, navy blue, pale blue, and snowy white undulating over green hills have inspired artists for decades.

Tudor girls made lavender tea to spur visions of their future husbands, and newlyweds stuffed lavender into their mattresses to inspire marital bliss.

A Favorite Herb through the Ages

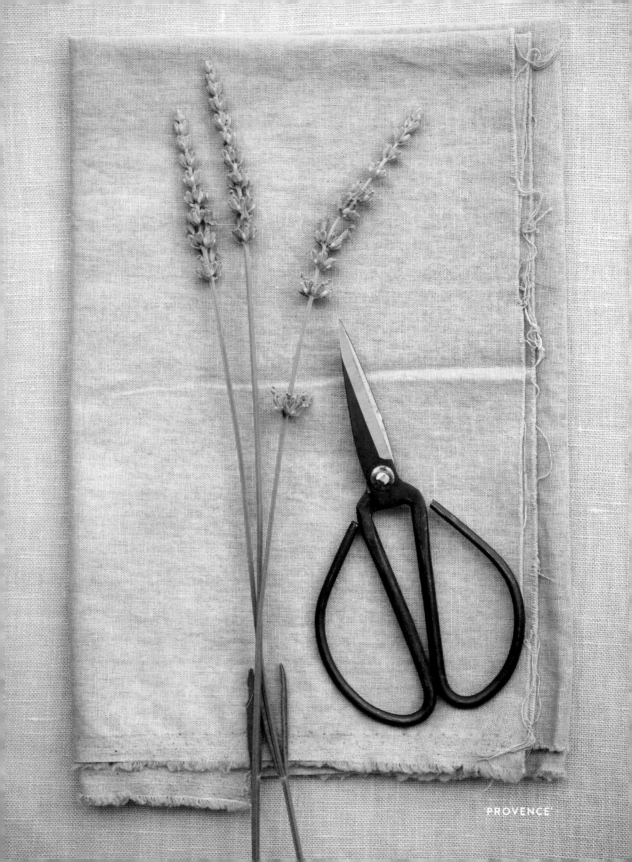

'PROVENCE'

1
learn about
LAVENDER

You might be surprised to learn that there are nearly 50 species of lavender with more than 450 varieties! Depending on how you want to use it—for color or fragrance, for cooking and baking, to attract bees and butterflies—you have hundreds of options.

What's in a Name?

Among the lavender family, there is a large range of plant sizes, colors, even scents. A few of the more well-known types are:

Lavandula angustifolia, commonly known as English lavender or true lavender

Lavandula dentata, sometimes referred to as French lavender

Lavandula × intermedia, a hybrid lavender

Lavandula stoechas, often referred to as Spanish lavender

It can be very confusing to try to understand the naming conventions of lavender, as the names often do not directly correlate to where the plant comes from. For example, French lavender does not always refer to lavender grown in France, and a label of Spanish lavender doesn't indicate that that variety was grown in Spain.

For simplicity's sake, here is a brief introduction to the three varieties grown on our farm, along with a few other favorite cultivars. If you're interested in a deeper dive into lavender varieties, there are many great resources out there. (See page 155 for a few suggestions.)

Egyptian hieroglyphics indicate that lavender was used in the mummification process. When the tomb of the Egyptian pharaoh Tutankhamun—King Tut—was opened, there were still traces of lavender fragrance. He died in 1323 BCE.

Lavandula angustifolia

Lavandula dentata

Lavandula × intermedia

Lavandula stoechas

Culinary or Regular?

LAVENDER AND LINALOOL

Lavender's calming effect comes from linalool, one of 200 compounds found in the herb. A Japanese study found that linalool acts as an anxiolytic to soothe anxiety, while other research shows that linalool can even help reverse the progression of some neurological disorders.

People often wonder what the difference is between culinary and regular lavender, and if they can be used interchangeably. Generally, lavender contains over 200 compounds that make up individual flavor and pharmaceutical profiles. Higher percentages of one compound, like linalool, dictate a particular lavender variety's character and usability for an intended purpose.

Most lavender aficionados agree that English lavender (*L. angustifolia*) is the best culinary lavender. These varieties are generally sweeter, milder, and richer in linalool and are also more floral than varieties with stronger camphor and woody scents, like Provence lavender. But like wine grape varieties, there are so many great culinary lavenders with individual flavor profiles—it's up to your personal taste.

One word about culinary vs. nonculinary: Since lavender is an herb, like mint, technically it's all edible, and people have been using culinary and nonculinary lavenders interchangeably for years. However, new research suggests that many of the Spanish and some of the intermedia lavender varieties have camphor and other strong terpenes that can be irritating to stomach and digestive tracts. Complaints from mild stomachache to cardiac incidents have been reported from Spanish lavender consumption.

For making teas and infusions, cooking, and baking, it's best to use tried-and-true culinary varieties of lavender.

All lavender is edible but some varieties are more suited to culinary uses than others.

On the Farm

Because our focus is cooking and baking with lavender and making wellness products, we chose varieties that not only offer wonderful aroma but also add delectable flavor. We grow 'Royal Velvet' and 'Provence', two culinary lavenders, for use in food recipes. 'Grosso', which produces exquisite essential oil, goes into our home and wellness products.

Lavandula angustifolia 'Royal Velvet'

FLOWER COLOR velvety dark navy/purple

FOLIAGE COLOR silver green

GOOD FOR cooking, crafts

'Royal Velvet' is hands down my favorite lavender. This little beauty is small—growing about 2 feet high—but it's mighty when it comes to confectionery value. We make all our lavender sugar and lavender salt grinders from 'Royal Velvet'. It offers a sweet, soft fragrance and a similarly pleasant, mild flavor.

GOOD MEDICINE

Legend has it that sixteenth-century French glovemakers perfumed gloves with lavender to ward off cholera, and grave-robbing thieves washed in the herb to avoid the plague.

FRESH

DRIED

Lavandula × intermedia 'Provence'

FLOWER COLOR pale lilac

FOLIAGE COLOR silver green

GOOD FOR cooking

In seventeenth-century London, wearing a small bunch of lavender on one's wrist was believed to prevent cholera.

Perhaps the most famous culinary lavender variety, 'Provence' is widely grown in the—you guessed it—Provence region of France, where it is coveted by local cooks whose kitchen talents turn 'Provence' lavender into haute cuisine. Thanks to a lavender-forward flavor profile, this cultivar shows up in honey infusions, olive oils, brines, savory dishes, and more. We use every single flower of our 'Provence' lavender each year! It anchors staple recipes like Lavender Honey, Lavender Lemon Pepper, Peppender dry spice, and numerous herb and spice blends.

FRESH

DRIED

Lavandula × *intermedia* 'Grosso'

FLOWER COLOR dark blue and purple, almost navy blue

FOLIAGE COLOR gray-green

GOOD FOR essential oil, sachets

This French hybrid is one of the highest producers of lavender essential oil as it's richer in camphor, linalool, and other terpenes than English lavender varieties. We use 'Grosso' for our farm-crafted lavender soaps, inhalers, essential oil rollers, and stress sticks.

FRESH

DRIED

Nearly all varieties of lavender offer a pleasing fragrance, but if you're looking for the most *fragrant, give these a try: 'Folgate', 'Grosso', 'Melissa', and 'Royal Velvet'.*

Some Other Excellent Cultivars

Here are a few more lavender cultivars that are worth experimenting with, either buying the buds or growing the plants yourself. (See Chapter 4 for the basics of growing lavender.)

Lavandula angustifolia 'Betty's Blue'

FLOWER COLOR dark blue

FOLIAGE COLOR gray-green

GOOD FOR crafts

Its small, tight flower heads make 'Betty's Blue' perfect for creating wreaths, braids, and other crafts, and its unique color adds a bright flair to dried bouquets. Fellow lavender growers have told us they love 'Betty's Blue' whenever their craft projects call for a variety that holds flower color and buds after drying.

Lavandula angustifolia 'Buena Vista'

FLOWER COLOR deep purple

FOLIAGE COLOR green

GOOD FOR cooking, gardening

'Buena Vista' blooms in spring and late summer, so it's a great choice if you're looking for a season-long flowering lavender for your garden. Plus, its flavor profile and wonderful scent are perfect for teas, especially lavender mint herbal tea.

Lavandula angustifolia 'Folgate'

FLOWER COLOR periwinkle blue

FOLIAGE COLOR gray-green

GOOD FOR culinary

Like 'Buena Vista', 'Folgate'—which flowers early—is a favorite among cooks. We love its flavor profile. It's a perfect confectionery lavender (along with 'Royal Velvet'), and we are adding it to new plantings here. Try its subtle flavor of sweet mint in pastries and other baked goods, syrups, and marinades, or blended into soft cheeses.

Lavandula angustifolia 'Melissa'

FLOWER COLOR pink and white

FOLIAGE COLOR green

GOOD FOR culinary, essential oil

'Melissa' is both a culinary lavender and one that's nice for essential oil production. This cultivar offers slight spice along with a hint of vanilla in both its taste and aroma, making a uniquely sweet, fragrant plant. We use it dried, crushed, and mixed with thyme and salt for a delicious rub on pork roasts. And we also love it for its beautiful color when the flowers are fresh.

Lavandula angustifolia 'Maillette'

FLOWER COLOR rich purple

FOLIAGE COLOR gray-green

GOOD FOR essential oil

This variety is predominantly cultivated in Provence, France, and is considered one of the best English lavenders for essential oil production thanks to its high quality and desirable aroma—slight floral, sweetly herbaceous notes with a subtle woody undertone.

Lavandula angustifolia 'Munstead'

FLOWER COLOR cool blue to rosy purple

FOLIAGE COLOR gray-green

GOOD FOR culinary, crafts

This lavender is widely grown and favored for its flowers that last throughout the entire growing season. With its rich flavor, 'Munstead' shines in any recipe, from sweets to soups. We also like it for herb blends and sugar infusions, as well as wreaths and dried flower arrangements. If you can only grow one lavender variety, 'Munstead' should be high on your list.

'FOLGATE'

'MELISSA'

MAILLETTE

'MUNSTEAD'

Lavandula angustifolia 'Purple Bouquet'

FLOWER COLOR dark, velvety lilac

FOLIAGE COLOR gray-green

GOOD FOR gardening, crafts

A long-stemmed, twice-blooming lavender, 'Purple Bouquet' boasts a fresh scent and hardy stems, making it ideal for crafting fresh or dried arrangements or planting to adorn a garden walkway.

Lavandula angustifolia 'Royal Purple'

FLOWER COLOR deep purple

FOLIAGE COLOR green

GOOD FOR gardening

This is a top choice for planting as a hedge or in an herb garden because of its elegant, long stems; sweet fragrance; and vibrantly colored flowers. It blooms once in early summer but may have a second, smaller flush later in the season, if trimmed to within three inches of the woody stem. The weather also has to cooperate to trigger the plants' natural regrowth cycle!

Lavandula × chaytorae 'Ana Luisa'

FLOWER COLOR blue-purple

FOLIAGE COLOR white to silver

GOOD FOR crafts, gardening

Notable for its white, wooly foliage, this hybrid enjoys a long growing season, making it ideal for year-round gardens and hedges that need a pop of color.

Lavandula × intermedia 'Edelweiss'

FLOWER COLOR white with blue-tinted flower buds

FOLIAGE COLOR green

GOOD FOR culinary

Our friends and fellow Arizona lavender farmers Bryan and Cindy Schooley at Windy Hills Lavender Farm in Heber introduced us to 'Edelweiss'. We are so glad they did! As a chef, Bryan prizes 'Edelweiss' for its lovely flavor and sweet scent. We are always on the hunt for those special lavender varieties to perfect our cooking and baking products, and 'Edelweiss' immediately made the cut.

'EDELWEISS'

Shades of Lavender

A natural mix of colors in a garden or field is always beautiful.
However, it can also be fun to coordinate shades and hues, too. Here's a snapshot
of where a few varieties fall on the lavender color wheel.

'PHENOMENAL'

'FOLGATE'

'BETTY'S BLUE'

'HIDCOTE'

The Blues

'Betty's Blue,'
'Blue Cushion', 'Hidcote',
and 'Violet Intrigue'

The Purples

'Folgate','Imperial Gem',
'Impress Purple', 'Phenomenal',
and 'Purple Bouquet'

Learn about Lavender

'MELISSA'

'PROVENCE'

'EDELWEISS'

The Lilacs

'Provence'

The Pinks

'Coconut Ice', 'Hidcote Pink',
'Little Lottie', and 'Melissa'

The Whites

'Edelweiss' and
'Melissa'

2
LAYERING LAVENDER
into your life

One of the best things about lavender is that it's so multifaceted. There are many ways to invite lavender into the everyday—inhaling its fragrance, sipping tea, hanging sachets in your closets. All these little efforts offer big payoffs. Lavender helps create an environment that enhances your overall well-being. Introducing lavender into your personal routine is so simple and yet yields wonderful restorative results.

This chapter shares ideas and inspiration, along with recipes to help you bring the joy, beauty, and benefits of lavender into your home and life.

BODY CARE:
relax, unwind, breathe deep

*From adding fragrance to a soothing bath to cleansing
your skin with antiseptic benefits, lavender offers easy and
impactful ways to bring about daily relaxation.*

Sugar Scrub

Sugar is one of the best natural ingredients for skin exfoliation, and this scrub is sure to keep you feeling radiant. You can use this lavender sugar scrub on your face, hands, and feet, or any part of your body that you want to feel silky and soft.

Although coconut oil is a popular DIY sugar scrub ingredient, it's highly comedogenic, which means it can clog skin pores and cause breakouts. High-quality grapeseed oil is a gentler choice. We like to add tea tree essential oil to this recipe; it's antibacterial and is great for cleansing, but you can leave it out.

Makes approximately 1 cup

materials

- 1¼ cups granulated sugar (or sugar of your choice)
- ¼ cup grapeseed oil
- 1 tablespoon sweet almond oil
- 1 tablespoon vegetable glycerin
- ½ teaspoon vitamin E oil
- 20 drops lavender essential oil
- 2 drops tea tree essential oil (optional)

to make

Measure each ingredient into a medium bowl and stir until thoroughly combined. Spoon into glass or plastic jars with tight-fitting lids. Use within 6 months.

to use

Massage a handful onto wet skin and exfoliate in circular motions. Rinse off with warm water and pat skin dry.

SKIN REVITALIZER

Lavender essential oil is an antibacterial, antimicrobial essential oil that is great for skin. When used topically, it's been shown to treat acne and other superficial skin conditions and may even fade age spots. In a sugar scrub, it offers exfoliating and skin-conditioning properties.

Wellness Soak

There's nothing like a lovely, long soak in a lavender bath to improve skin health and hydration, and to relieve mild skin conditions like itchiness or eczema. It also helps ease muscle soreness and joint pain.

Makes approximately 3 cups

The Romans bathed in lavender, one of the earliest examples of people embracing the herb's fresh fragrance in their daily routines. The Romans were also the ones to name the herb, deriving it from the Latin verb *lavare*, meaning "to wash."

materials

- 1 cup baking soda
- 2 cups Epsom salt
- ½ cup Himalayan salt
- 10–12 drops lavender essential oil
- 1 tablespoon fresh lavender (optional)

to make

1 Mix the baking soda, Epsom salt, and Himalayan salt in a large bowl. Add the lavender essential oil, a few drops at a time, stirring thoroughly to incorporate the oil.

2 Add the fresh lavender, if using, and stir again.

3 Let the mixture sit uncovered for up to 90 minutes, or until the oil is fully absorbed. The mixture must be thoroughly dry before being stored or it will harden. Store in a sealed container for up to 6 months.

to use

Stir ½ to 2 cups into a warm bath and enjoy!

Face Wash

This face wash cleans skin with lavender's antiseptic properties while serving as a form of aromatherapy to help soothe stress and anxiety. Lavender essential oil pairs with tea tree essential oil and honey to exfoliate, fight bacteria, and soften skin. Using this wash is a great way to start and end your day.

Makes approximately 8 ounces

materials

- ½ cup distilled water, warmed to about 105°F (40°C)
- 3 tablespoons raw honey
- ½ cup pure castile liquid soap (we like Dr. Bronner's)
- 2 teaspoons avocado oil or argan, jojoba, or grapeseed oil
- ¼ teaspoon lavender essential oil
- 5 drops tea tree essential oil
- 5 drops vitamin E oil
- 3 drops vitamin C serum with 20% hyaluronic acid*

8-ounce glass or plastic pump bottle or two 4-ounce ones

*Readily available at major retailers and online

We recommend using Certified Naturally Grown (CNG) or organic ingredients for all your made-at-home lavender products.

to make

1 Pour the warm water into a clean bowl and add the honey. Stir until the honey is completely dissolved.

2 Add the liquid soap, avocado oil, lavender and tea tree essential oils, vitamin E, and vitamin C. Whisk to combine.

3 Pour the mixture into the storage container and secure the lid tightly. (I like to use two smaller bottles; one for home and one for my travel bag.) Label and date the containers. Store in a cool, dry place and use within 1 year.

to use

Wet your face with warm water. Shake the bottle and apply a quarter-size amount of the face wash to your hands. Gently rub it into your face, neck, and décolletage with the pads of your fingers, using circular motions. Take a moment to cup your hands over your face and nose and breathe in a few times for a mini aromatherapy session!

Rinse thoroughly with warm water and pat dry.

Face Oil

Thanks to its anti-inflammatory properties and antioxidants, lavender can help reduce dry skin, redness, and puffiness. This face oil will make your skin soft, supple, and glowing, without clogging pores.

Makes approximately 1 ounce

materials

- 3 teaspoons argan oil
- 1 teaspoon hempseed oil
- 1 teaspoon grapeseed oil
- ¼ teaspoon rosehip oil
- 10 drops lavender essential oil
- 5 drops carrot seed oil
- 4 drops vitamin E oil
- 2 drops lemon oil

    1-ounce, dark-glass bottle with a dropper lid, or glass or plastic pump bottle

to make

Measure each ingredient into a small bowl and stir until thoroughly combined. Using a funnel, pour the mixture into the bottle. Label and date the bottle. Use within 6 months.

to use

Wash your face thoroughly. Shake the bottle and apply a few drops of face oil to your fingertips. Massage into your forehead, cheeks, and neck until the oil is absorbed. Repeat daily. This product can be kept in the shower for easy access.

PEACE OF MIND

Lavender can lessen some symptoms of anxiety, such as impaired sleep and decreased quality of life. A study published in the *World Journal of Biological Psychiatry* reported that Silexan, a lavender oil available in 80 mg capsules for relief of anxiety, provided a calming effect to patients with generalized anxiety disorder after two weeks of use.

Lavender Essential Oil

Listed here are just a few of the dozens of ways to use lavender essential oil to help you reap its calming benefits. And it only takes a few drops— essential oils are highly concentrated, so use as directed. Be sure you're sourcing quality oil, extracted from lavender Certified Naturally Grown (CNG) at or above 5,000 feet elevation. Growing lavender at higher altitudes increases the production and accumulation of terpenes.

• Add 1 or 2 drops to warm bathwater for a soothing soak.

• Use a diffuser to disperse the scent throughout a room.

• Add 3 drops to a cool washcloth or cold compress to reduce headache pain.

• Make an aromatherapy and sanitizing spray by adding 5 drops lavender essential oil and 2 teaspoons witch hazel to 1 cup distilled water—great for pet beds, cars, and anywhere you want the fresh scent of lavender. It's also excellent for soothing sunburn and other skin irritations.

• Fill an aromatherapy inhaler so you can enjoy the olfactory power of lavender on the go. Disposable nasal inhalers are readily available online. Soak the provided wick with about 15 drops lavender essential oil or your favorite blend of oils. To de-stress, simply breathe in the scent.

• To freshen and lightly scent linens, put 12 drops lavender essential oil on a clean white sock. Tie the sock tightly around the oily spot to prevent it from staining other fabric. Toss the knotted sock in the dryer with your sheets and towels.

Hand-harvesting lavender for oil distillation is a small-farm passion, just like plucking grapes by hand for a superior final product is at great small-batch wineries. Varietal lavender essential oil is much like varietals in wine, with distinct fragrance and compound profiles. Seek out specific varietal lavender essential oils from quality farms and decide for yourself which ones you love best. As in wine, blends can be very good, too.

Though the research suggests that lavender offers many health benefits, please note that the FDA doesn't monitor or regulate the purity or quality of essential oils. You should always check with your doctor or healthcare advisor before treating any medical condition with any essential oil.

Bath Bombs

This is a fail-safe bath bomb recipe, but the secret is in following the exact measurements. You can make these on your own, but it's also fun to invite a few friends over. Traditional bath bomb molds in all sorts of shapes are available online, but you can use cupcake pans, teacups, extra-large ice cube trays—whatever works for you! At the farm, we love the shapes and sizes from using a moon pie press (pictured here). You can make these any size you like, but about 6 ounces of material is a good amount per bomb.

Makes 4 or 5 bath bombs, depending on size and shape of mold

materials

- 1 cup baking soda
- ½ cup cornstarch
- ½ cup citric acid
- ½ cup + 2 tablespoons Epsom salt
- 2 tablespoons grapeseed oil
- 1 tablespoon witch hazel or rubbing alcohol
- 1 teaspoon lavender essential oil
- Pinch of dried lavender buds (optional)

to use

Fill your tub with warm water, drop in one bath bomb, and enjoy the fragrance of lavender as it dissolves into the water around you. Bath bombs make a wonderful foot soak, too: deodorizing, softening, and healing. Foot skin is typically less sensitive, so use a whole bomb for efficacy and to be sure you can enjoy the relaxing fragrance. Use within 1 year.

SHOWER STEAMER

If you don't have time for a soak in the tub, turn a bath bomb into a shower steamer (also called a shower fizzie) to deliver the same aromatherapy benefits. Place one bath bomb in a spot in your shower where the hot water can dissolve it and vaporize the lavender scent to reduce stress and calm anxiety.

To add color to your bath bomb, use skin-safe mica powder pigments. Start with ⅛ teaspoon of mica for a lighter color and build from there to achieve the desired hue. Keep in mind: The more pigment you use, the higher the possibility of tub and skin staining.

1 Thoroughly mix the baking soda, cornstarch, citric acid, and Epsom salt in a medium bowl.

2 Add the grapeseed oil, witch hazel, and lavender essential oil. Mix well.

3 Add the lavender buds, if using, and mix again.

4 Press the mixture tightly into the molds— just hand pressure is sufficient. The idea is to remove air pockets and compress the ingredients so they bind as they dry.

5 Remove the bombs gently from the molds and set aside to dry thoroughly, approximately 12 hours, before handling or wrapping.

Massage oil makes a
lovely gift presented
in a beautiful recycled
glass bottle capped with
a cork. Tie on a pretty
label with colorful ribbon
and tuck in a stem of
dried lavender.

Bath and Massage Oil

We sell countless bottles of lavender bath oil and can testify firsthand that in addition to its ability to calm, relax, and soothe, lavender produces a powerhouse essential oil that's great for softening skin.

But don't limit this wonderful lavender oil to just the bath! It's a perfect massage oil and after-shower moisturizer, and it's amazing when added to a footbath, too.

Makes 8 ounces

materials

8 ounces fresh grapeseed oil

½ teaspoon lavender essential oil (we use 'Grosso')

4 or 5 sprigs of dried lavender

8-ounce bottle with cork or lid

to make

1 Pour the grapeseed oil into a small bowl and add the lavender essential oil, then stir well.

2 Drop the lavender stems into the bottle, trimming to fit as needed. Using a funnel, fill the bottle with the lavender essential oil and grapeseed oil mixture, covering the lavender stems. Seal the bottle.

to use

To use as a bath oil, pour the desired amount into the tub while the water is running. To use as a massage oil, apply oil to your hands and rub gently into the skin to massage and moisturize. Shake before using to redisperse the essential oil.

Store in a cool, dark spot and use within 6 months.

Beard Oil

This beard oil softens and conditions both hair and skin. Customers have told us they like to massage it into their beards at night to help them sleep.

Makes approximately 1 ounce

materials

2 teaspoons argan oil or grapeseed oil

2 teaspoons jojoba oil

1½ teaspoons hempseed oil

10 drops lavender essential oil

8 drops rosemary essential oil

5 drops patchouli essential oil

3 drops vitamin E oil

1-ounce, dark-glass bottle with a dropper lid, or a glass or plastic pump bottle

to make

Measure each ingredient into a small bowl and stir until thoroughly combined. Using a funnel, pour the mixture into the bottle. Label and date the bottle. Use within 1 year.

to use

Shake the bottle well and place 2 or 3 drops on your fingertips. Massage into clean beard and skin. This product can be kept in the shower for easy access.

HEALTHY HAIR

Lavender can treat hair loss when applied topically on the scalp. A study published by the National Center for Biotechnology Information indicated that when combined with the essential oils from thyme, rosemary, and cedarwood, lavender essential oil may improve hair growth by as much as 44 percent over seven months.

Lavender Rollerball

An aromatherapy rollerball is a vial fitted with a roller applicator, and it's typically filled with a mixture of essential oils in a carrier oil, such as grapeseed oil, jojoba oil, or sweet almond oil. Refillable 10 ml dark-glass rollerball vials (preferably with plastic rollers) are available online and at major retailers.

You can use lavender essential oil alone or mix it with another essential oil to enhance the impact. We like these combinations: lavender and evening primrose for relaxation and stress relief and to enhance sleep, lavender and eucalyptus for help relieving sinus pressure, and lavender and peppermint for soothing headaches.

Simply add a few drops of each essential oil to the vial and top off with your choice of carrier oil. Cap the vial tightly and shake well to mix. To use, roll oil onto the forehead, temples, back of the neck, and upper lip and behind the ears.

Lavender Tea

Lavender tea is a powerful antioxidant and a way to make small changes that deliver big health benefits. Relieve the stress of the day and settle the brain for sleep with a cup of lavender herbal tea, hot or iced. Experiment with your favorite tea plus lavender to find the perfect combo for you. Caffeine-free combinations we like are lavender and mint or lavender and chamomile. To make: Fill a disposable loose-leaf tea bag or a tea infuser with dried herbs and steep for a few minutes in hot water. Sweeten with Lavender Honey (page 78), if desired.

SWEET SLEEP

The inhalation of lavender aids sleep. That's because its compounds activate the parasympathetic system, which generates a feeling of relaxation, according to a study at the Medical University of Taipei. How? It increases delta waves in slow-wave sleep—the stage where you sleep the deepest—and reduces alpha waves in the prefrontal region of the brain in wake-stage sleep.

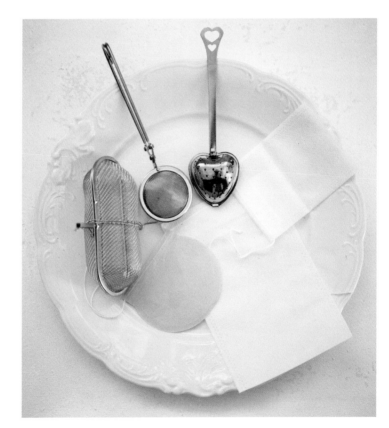

IN THE HOME
lavender all around

*Lavender's beauty can accent
every room of the home,
in a sweet bouquet on a coffee table,
a colorful herb braid in the kitchen,
or a welcoming wreath
on your front door.
No matter how you choose to enjoy
the scent and sight of lavender,
there's only one rule:
Get creative and have fun!*

Culinary Herb Braid

Our herb-braiding class is one of our most popular offerings on preserving farm-fresh lavender and herbs. The result is functional *and* gorgeous—your friends and family will be so grateful if you hand them out as gifts.

It's best to use fresh lavender and herbs for this project. I like to use different colors and varieties of culinary lavender for a more interesting braid. You can tuck in any dried herbs, garlic bulbs, and dried chiles to add to the flavors and visual appeal.

Any edible herb or flower is fair game. Some suggestions are rosemary, lovage, thyme, dill, mint, red basil, sage, dandelions, and small pink and red tea roses. Just make sure they will dry well and not fade too quickly. For example, chives stems become unusably tough, but the flowers are a pretty addition.

materials

6–12 feet of multistrand raffia or heavy cotton rope, cut into three equal lengths

About 500 stems of culinary lavender, 6–8 inches long

Small rubber bands, preferably beige

About 150 stems of culinary herbs, several different types, 4–6 inches long

Small onions, garlic bulbs, dried chiles (optional)

Twine or small-gauge floral wire

6-inch piece of heavy string or wire

Approximately 36 inches of burlap wire-edge ribbon or raffia (optional)

NOTE: You are working with fresh material, so it's important that the herbs have sufficient air around them during the drying process. Band the herbs loosely to create the individual bundles. We create our lavender braids in summer when it's warm and dry outside. A general rule is to make sure your braids are dry to the touch within 72 hours, which gives them little chance of developing mold. If you're making the braids in humid conditions or the flowers are wet or dewy, allow 3-inch bundles to air-dry for a full day before braiding.

Also, keep in mind where the braid will hang. For example, if you plan to have it on a wall, work with your braid on a flat surface to keep the flower bunches on the same plane where they will be exposed to the air while they dry.

continued on next page

1   Double the strands of raffia and make a loop at the top. Separate the strands as shown to make it easier to attach the lavender and herbs.

2   Depending on the size of your braid, make 12 to 15 bundles of fresh lavender, each containing 20 to 30 stems. Arrange the stems with the flowers pointing in the same direction. Secure the stems with a small rubber band and trim evenly.

3   Make 8 to 10 bundles of other fresh herbs, using 8 to 12 stems of each herb to create 3- to 4-inch-wide bunches. Secure the stem ends with a small rubber band and trim evenly.

4 Tie one or two lavender bunches to the bottom of each rafia strand, hiding the ends of the raffia.

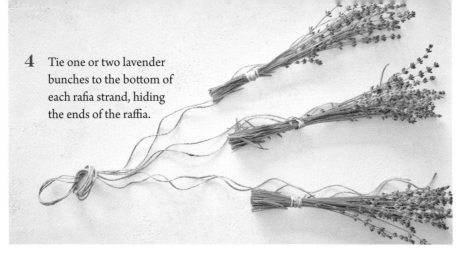

5 Alternate adding bunches of herbs and lavender to each strand, securing them with floral wire or twine.

6   Cover each strand to the top, creating a combination that you'll love to hang in your kitchen. You can add roses or other edible flowers for visual appeal. Braid the finished strands together, being careful not to plait them too tightly.

7   Sometimes I fill in blank spots with dried onions, garlic bulbs, or dried chiles. They can be secured using their stems or tucked into tight spaces where they will be held by surrounding foliage.

8   Wrap the bottom end of the braid with another heavy rubber band or several rounds of wire. Make a 2-inch loop from heavy twine or wire to use as the hanger for the braid and secure it into the top wire or rubber band of the braid. If you want, add a bow, securing with twine or wire.

9   Hang the braid in a dry, airy place out of direct light where you can enjoy your beautiful, preserved herbs in your favorite recipes and teas!

Lavender Sachet Mix

We use this mix to fill sachets and eye pillows (directions follow). You can make sachets in any size, shape, and fabric to use where you desire the scent of lavender. Add to dresser drawers, pet beds, and closets, or attach a pretty ribbon loop to hang the sachet in your car. The possibilities are endless!

Makes 4 cups

materials

- 1 cup dried lavender buds
- 1 cup plain white rice (not an aromatic variety like jasmine or basmati)
- 2 cups organic buckwheat hulls

to make

Mix all ingredients together thoroughly. Store the unused portion in a tightly sealed plastic bag, removing as much air as possible to preserve the fragrance. Use within 2 years.

Whatever you use this sachet mixture for, it's important to give the mixture a squeeze from time to time to bring the lavender essential oil back to the surface and reinvigorate the scent.

Sachet

A sachet is *the* product for bringing the calming properties of lavender into your home. You can put a sachet anywhere: inside shoes, drawers, car consoles, purses, gym bags, luggage, pet beds, or even as a dryer bag to drop in with your laundry. The sachet mix on page 52 makes enough to fill sixteen 3-inch square sachet bags, but you can adjust the directions to make the bags any size you desire.

materials

Fabric-marking tool and ruler

Two 3½-inch squares of cotton or linen fabric

Pins

Thread

¼ cup Lavender Sachet Mix (page 52) or all lavender buds

Pinking shears

to make

Use a ⅜-inch seam allowance throughout.

1 Mark a 2-inch opening on the right side of your top fabric piece. This opening is where you will insert the sachet mix.

continued on next page

Sachet *continued*

2   Place the squares with wrong sides together, lining up the raw edges. Pin. Starting at one opening mark, and pivoting at corners, machine stitch around the edges until you reach the other opening mark. Reinforce with extra backstitching at each end of the opening.

3   Fill the sachet with the sachet mix. Sew the opening closed on a machine. Backstitch at the beginning and the end.

To amp up the lavender impact, replace the sachet mix with 100 percent dried lavender buds. And to keep it even simpler, skip sewing a bag. Instead, put dried lavender in a premade organza bag and tie it shut with ribbon.

4   Using pinking shears, trim the edges of the finished sachet by ¼ inch.

Hanging Sachet

By adding a loop made of ribbon, your sachet can hang anywhere. To add a decorative touch, it's fun to vary lavender prints on one side of the sachet with contrasting fabric on the other side.

¼-inch-wide × 8-inch-long ribbon

Two 4- × 6-inch pieces of cotton or linen fabric

Pins

Needle

Thread

Tailor's chalk or fabric-marking tool

Scissors

1 cup Lavender Sachet Mix (page 52)

to make

Use a ½-inch seam allowance unless otherwise indicated.

1 The ribbon loop is sewn on the right side of one piece of fabric at one short end; this will become the "top" of the sachet. The end opposite the loop will be the "bottom." Pin the ends of the ribbon to the raw edge of the fabric ½ inch apart.

2   The hanger will be upside down. Baste the ends of the ribbon to the fabric using a ¼-inch seam allowance.

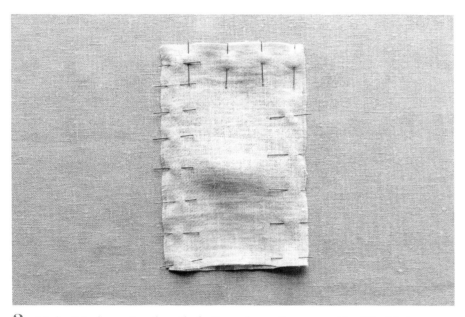

3   Mark a 2-inch opening along the bottom edge on the wrong side of the fabric. Pin the right sides of the fabric together. The ribbon loop will be sandwiched between the sides of the sachet.

continued on next page

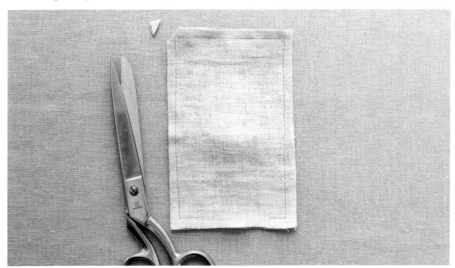

4   Starting at one end of the opening mark, machine stitch around the edges with a
½-inch seam allowance, pivoting at the corners. Reinforce well with extra backstitching
at each end of the opening. Square off the corners by trimming the seam allowances
at a 45-degree angle, but be careful to avoid cutting too close to the stitching.

5   Turn the sachet right side out. Fill with 1 cup of sachet mix. Tuck the opening seam
allowances to the inside of the sachet. Sew the opening shut, either on your machine
or by hand.

In medieval France, women who washed clothes for hire were called lavenders.

Eye Pillow

A lavender eye pillow makes unwinding after a long day so easy. To soothe tired eyes and lull you into sleepy time, you can warm the pillow in the microwave for 30 seconds or store it in the freezer for cooling relief. A lavender eye pillow is also great as a cold pack for strained muscles.

Makes 1 pillow

materials

Two 5- × 10-inch pieces of cotton fabric

Tailor's chalk or fabric-marking tool

Sewing ruler

Pins

Needle and thread

Scissors

½–1 cup Lavender Sachet Mix (page 52)

to make

Use a ¼-inch seam allowance throughout.

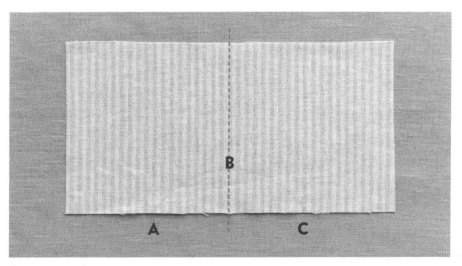

1 The bottom of the eye pillow is sewn with a crescent shape that is 1¾ × 4 inches. To create this curved seamline, mark the center of one long edge of the fabric on the wrong side. Measure and mark 2 inches to the left of the center (point A) and 2 inches to the right (point C). Measure ¾ inches up from this center (point B) and make a mark. Draw an arc that connects points A, B, and C.

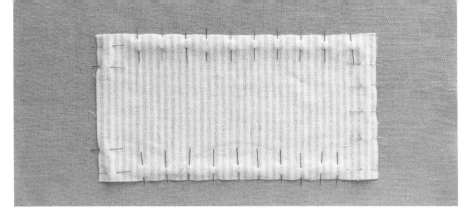

2   On the wrong side of one short end, mark a 2-inch opening. Pin the fabric with right sides together.

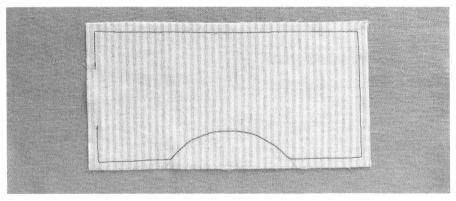

3   Starting at one end of the opening mark and pivoting at corners, machine stitch around the edges. Reinforce well with extra backstitching at each end of the opening.

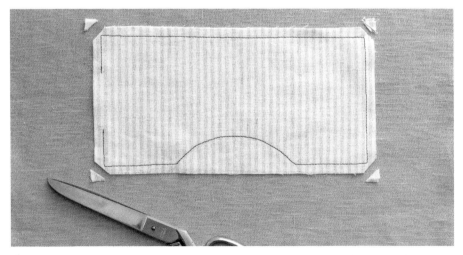

4   Square off the corners by trimming the seam allowances at a 45-degree angle. Avoid cutting too close to the stitching.

continued on next page

Eye Pillow *continued*

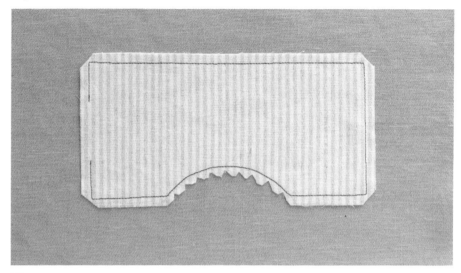

5   Trim the curved bottom edge by ⅛ inch and cut small V-shaped wedges into the seam allowance to remove bulk and allow the seam allowances to open up and lie flat.

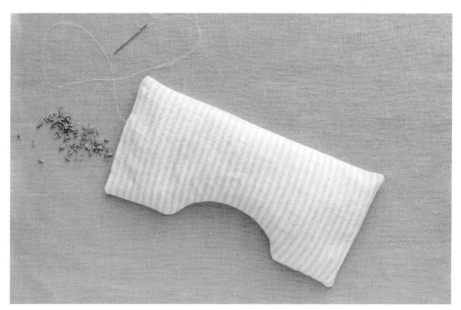

6   Turn the pillow right side out. Fill with the sachet mix. Don't overfill; you want the pillow to lie comfortably on your face. Tuck the opening seam allowances to the inside of the sachet. Using thread and a needle, slipstitch the opening closed.

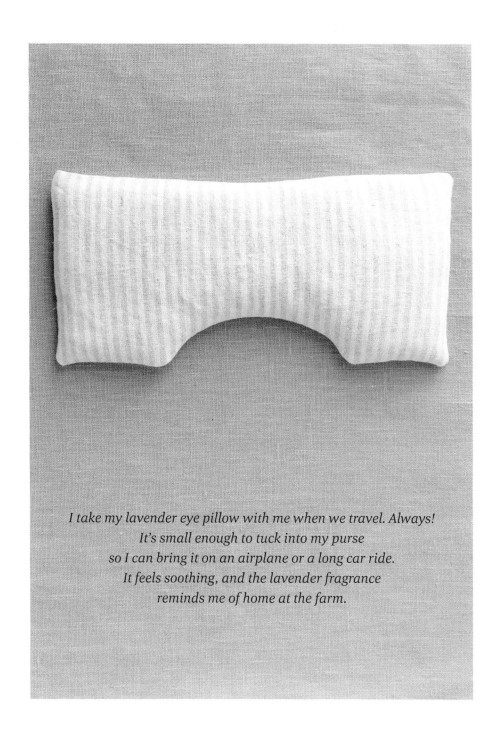

I take my lavender eye pillow with me when we travel. Always!
It's small enough to tuck into my purse
so I can bring it on an airplane or a long car ride.
It feels soothing, and the lavender fragrance
reminds me of home at the farm.

Lavender Spa Mist

In many unwinding practices, like yoga and meditation, triggering the brain to recognize a specific scent, such as lavender, helps cue relaxation. Research shows that the scent activates the parasympathetic nervous system to generate a feeling of tranquility and relaxation. This lavender mist can help you bypass the chaos of daily life.

Makes 8 ounces

materials

- 4 ounces distilled water (½ cup)
- 4 ounces lavender hydrosol (½ cup)
  8-ounce spray bottle
- 25 drops lavender essential oil (¼ teaspoon)

to make

Using a funnel, pour the distilled water and hydrosol into the spray bottle. Add the lavender essential oil. Shake well to blend. Store in a cool spot and use within 6 months.

to use

Shake well and spritz lightly anywhere you wish to create an aromatherapy spa experience. Avoid spraying directly on materials that might be stained by the oil.

All About Hydrosol

Hydrosol is the scented water produced when distilling plant materials such as fresh flowers, leaves, and fruits. It contains no essential oil and therefore won't stain fabrics. Lavender hydrosol, also known as lavender linen spray, has a host of great wellness benefits. You can purchase hydrosol from lavender farms, online herbal resources, and wellness stores.

In addition to its aromatherapy benefits, lavender hydrosol can be used to cleanse skin, treat and soothe acne and rosacea, cool sunburned skin, and condition hair.

DRIED LAVENDER BOUQUET

Put a bouquet on your bedside table, use one as a centerpiece on your dining table,
set a bouquet on the windowsill, or tie a few with ribbons to give away to loved ones.
We think lavender is beautiful just as it is, but you can get
creative with your bouquet by weaving in other plants, flowers, and herbs.

'PROVENCE'   'ROYAL BLUE'   'MELISSA'   'ROYAL VELVET'

Spray Cleaner

As a cleaning product, lavender shines. Its powerful antibacterial, antiviral, and antifungal properties, boosted with the addition of tea tree essential oil, make it an effective and safe household cleaner.

Makes 8 ounces

materials

- 4 ounces distilled water (½ cup)
- 4 ounces white vinegar (½ cup)
- 8-ounce clean, empty spray bottle
- 12–15 drops lavender essential oil (about ⅛ teaspoon)
- 4–6 drops tea tree essential oil

to make

Using a funnel, pour the distilled water and vinegar into the spray bottle. Add the lavender and tea tree essential oils. Shake well to blend. Store in a cool spot and use within 6 months.

to use

Use this lavender spray as your daily cleaning agent for everything from your yoga mat to countertops. Spray on a surface, then wipe with a clean, dry cloth or paper towel. Please note that this lavender spray cleaner is not FDA-approved as a sanitizer.

ANTIFUNGAL SUPERHERO

Lavender offers powerful antifungal properties. Data published in the *Journal of Medical Microbiology* indicated that lavender essential oil killed fungi in skin, hair, and nail infections.

Not Everyone Loves Lavender

Although it attracts pollinators en masse, we have found lavender to be a fairly effective deterrent for pests. We sell loads of lavender cuttings to people who use them for scorpion repellent around their homes, especially in the hot Phoenix summer. Customers tell us it works for them!

Many of them also credit pots of 'Grosso' lavender sitting by their entry doors for keeping flies and mosquitoes to a minimum. We use bags of ground lavender stems in every barn and storage area, including our pantry, to repel crawling creatures of all varieties, including mice.

In our experience, lavender works well but isn't perfect! We tell customers that lavender is a deterrent, but it's not equal to commercial products. It's a trade-off between levels of effectiveness.

3

In the
KITCHEN
and on the table

With its herbaceous flavor and delectable scent, lavender has a long history as a culinary herb. A member of the mint family, it adds not only its wonderful flavor to foods but also heaping health benefits. It is hugely versatile and can be infused into honey, teas, and spirits; used in spice and herb mixes; added to dressings and marinades; and baked into a delectable assortment of sweets.

All lavender varieties are edible, but as noted previously, Spanish and intermedia cultivars might be irritating to some digestive systems. We recommend using only trusted culinary varieties such as 'Provence'. (See Chapter 1 for more about different varieties of lavender.)

PANTRY STAPLES

Creating great lavender dishes begins with having quality lavender staples in your kitchen. Many of the recipes you'll see here reference ingredients such as "Lavender Salt" or "Lavender Lemon Pepper." These delectable pantry staples are essential to making many of the dishes in this book.

We test all our recipes using only 'Provence' and 'Royal Velvet' lavenders, generally considered to be excellent culinary varieties. We recommend using Certified Naturally Grown (CNG) or organic lavender for consuming. Be sure to do your own research on food safety and toxicity if you're using unfamiliar lavender varieties or ones not mentioned in this book.

In addition to the pantry staples listed in this section, it might be a good idea to also have on hand 2 cups of confectionery lavender, such as 'Royal Velvet', 'Edelweiss', 'Melissa', 'Royal Blue', or 'Munstead', and 2 cups of dried culinary lavender buds, such as 'Provence', all stored in a sealed container in the pantry with your other herbs and spices for ready use.

Safe Storage Tips

Farm-crafted food is always the best. But without preservatives, the safe storage of these foods is key. Be sure to:

- Wash all containers in hot, soapy water and dry thoroughly before using for storage.

- Label and date all homemade products.

- Store dried herbs and seasonings in an airtight container in a cool, dry place. Use within a year.

- Store vinegars and oils in a cool, dark place. Use within 6 months.

- Refrigerate simple syrups and jams.

It's important to use freshly ground herbs and spices, so we recommend using refillable spice grinders to store the Lavender Himalayan Salt (page 72), Lavender Lemon Pepper (page 74), Peppender (page 75), and Lavender Herbes de Provence (page 73). Affordable grinders are available from many retailers that sell kitchen supplies.

Lavender Himalayan Salt

Lavender salt is delicious on roasted potatoes (page 101) and sweet potatoes tossed in lots of olive oil. It's also great on eggs, fish, salads, baked chicken, lavender chocolate, and hot buttered popcorn.

Makes 1¼ cups

ingredients

1 cup Himalayan salt

¼ cup 'Royal Velvet' dried lavender buds

to make

Mix the ingredients together, then pour them into a spice grinder. Store any remaining mixture in a sealed container away from heat and light for up to 1 year.

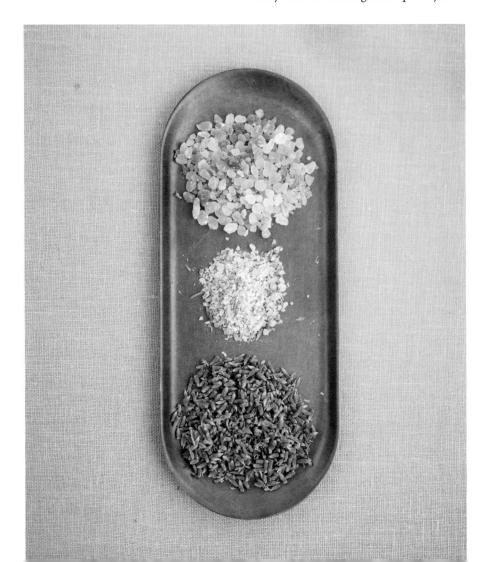

Lavender Herbes de Provence

There are many recipes for herbes de Provence, varying by region and chef. This blend uses both peppery 'Provence' lavender and sweeter, milder 'Royal Velvet' lavender, along with other fragrant herbs.

This versatile seasoning enhances soups and stews and is used extensively in meat and poultry dishes as a rub or marinade. Mixed with olive oil and vinegar, it's a delicious salad dressing. Try it drizzled on goat or feta cheeses or with olives and fresh tomato cubes.

Makes approximately ¾ cup

ingredients

¼ cup dried thyme

⅛ cup dried marjoram

⅛ cup dried summer savory

1 tablespoon dried tarragon

1 tablespoon dried sweet basil

1 teaspoon dried mint

⅛ cup 'Provence' dried lavender buds

⅛ cup 'Royal Velvet' dried lavender buds

to make

Mix all the herbs in a large bowl until well combined.

Store in a sealed container away from heat and light for up to 1 year.

Lavender Lemon Pepper

Once you grind this onto a bed of fresh greens, you'll never eat a salad without it. Try it on steaks, chops, and stir-fry dishes. It's a go-to, all-purpose kitchen necessity.

Makes approximately 2½ cups

ingredients

1 cup whole black peppercorns

½ cup 'Provence' dried lavender buds

½ cup chopped dried lemon peel

¼ cup dried onion flakes

¼ cup dried garlic granules

1 tablespoon Himalayan salt

to make

Measure each ingredient into a small bowl, mix, then pour into a spice grinder.

Store in a sealed container away from heat and light for up to 1 year.

Peppender

Although similar to Lavender Lemon Pepper (page 74), this pantry staple increases the amount of lavender and salt for a lavender-forward flavor that creates an amazing meat and vegetable rub. It's a wonderful all-purpose seasoning for everyday cooking that adds a punch of flavor anywhere you'd use regular pepper.

Makes approximately 1 cup

ingredients

- 1 cup + 1 tablespoon dried culinary lavender, any variety
- 1 cup whole black peppercorns
- ⅛ cup salt
- ½ cup chopped dried lemon peel
- ¼ cup dried onion flakes
- ¼ cup dried minced garlic

to make

Combine all ingredients in a high-speed blender. Blend on high until spices are reduced to a fine powder.

Store in a sealed container away from heat and light for up to 1 year.

Lavender Sugar

Use this sweetly scented sugar just as you would regular granulated sugar—
sub one to one. It's perfect for making scones, ice cream (page 117), and
sugar cookies and for sweetening beverages.

Makes approximately 2 cups

ingredients

2 cups granulated sugar

2 tablespoons 'Royal Velvet' dried
lavender buds

to make

1 Put the sugar in a high-speed blender.
Add the lavender buds and blend on
high for 25 to 30 seconds.

2 Shake down the ingredients and blend
for another 10 seconds, making sure
all the lavender has been incorporated
into the sugar.

Store in a sealed container away
from heat and light for up to 1 year.

Lavender Simple Syrup

Once you've tried the "lavenderized" version of a cocktail, like a margarita (page 121), this simple syrup will surely become one of your pantry staples. Substitute it anytime a recipe calls for simple syrup to bring a fabulous French flair to every sip.

Makes approximately 1 cup

ingredients

- 1 cup water
- 1 cup granulated sugar
- 3 tablespoons 'Royal Velvet' dried lavender buds

to make

1 Combine the water, sugar, and lavender buds in a nonreactive saucepan. Stir over medium heat until the sugar dissolves completely.

2 Reduce the heat to low and let sit for 12 to 15 minutes to allow the lavender buds to infuse into the sugar water.

3 Remove from the heat and let cool. Strain the lavender buds from the syrup.

Store in a sealed container in the refrigerator for up to 1 month.

VARIATION

If you have Lavender Sugar (page 76) on hand, an even quicker and easier method is to combine 1 cup lavender sugar and 1 cup water in a nonreactive pan. Heat over medium heat, mixing until the sugar dissolves. Remove from the heat and let cool before storing as above.

Lavender Honey

A Provençal must-have, this honey is the key ingredient of Sticky Lavender-Honey Chicken (page 85). Brush it on roasted sweet potatoes, swirl it into tea, and use it to make honey-roasted nuts. I love to assemble a plate of cheeses, fruits, and crackers, then dress the plate with drizzles of lavender honey.

Makes 1 pint

ingredients

- 1 pint glass jar of honey
- 2 tablespoons 'Provence' dried lavender buds

to make

1 Place the uncovered jar of honey in a pan of water. Heat the water over medium heat to about 105°F (40°C) and warm the honey until it liquefies.

2 When the honey is pourable, remove the jar from the heat and add the lavender buds. Stir to incorporate them thoroughly.

3 Tightly recap the jar and store it in a warm location. The buds will settle to the bottom of the jar, so every couple of days, turn the jar over to mix them into the honey again. After 1 to 2 weeks, taste the honey to see if it has developed the lavender flavor profile you desire. The warmer the room temperature, the faster the honey will infuse.

4 When you're satisfied with the flavor, warm the honey again in a pan of water over medium heat until it liquefies. Pour the honey into a clean, dry container through a fine-mesh strainer to remove the lavender buds.

Store at room temperature for up to 6 months. If crystals form on the bottom of the jar, simply reheat the honey in a pan of water over medium heat. Microwaving honey is not recommended.

Lavender Vinegars and Oils

Vinegars and oils offer a simple way to add the wonderful essence of lavender into your everyday recipes. These staples are so easy to make, I often double the recipe to make gifts for family and friends.

For lavender-infused vinegars, I like white balsamic or a quality apple cider vinegar. For infused oils, I recommend using a top-quality olive oil for salads and pastas and as a sauté or finishing oil. Use grapeseed or other high-temperature oils for added flavor while frying and searing.

Makes 1 pint

ingredients

- 1 pint of your favorite vinegar or olive oil
- 2 tablespoons 'Provence' dried lavender buds
- 1 pint dark-glass bottle with a tight-fitting screw lid or cork

to make

These instructions indicate vinegar throughout; for olive oil, follow the same steps.

1 Pour the vinegar into a pan and heat over medium-low heat until just warm, about 105°F (40°C).

2 Add the lavender buds to the pan and stir to distribute.

3 Let the mixture cool, then pour it into the bottle, using a funnel. Seal the bottle and store it in a convenient location. Shake it every 4 days, tasting to see if the vinegar has developed the flavor profile you desire. This process takes 1 to 2 weeks. The warmer the room temperature, the faster the flavor will infuse.

4 Once infused, pour the vinegar through a fine-mesh strainer to remove the lavender buds. Return the infusion to the bottle, then add a pretty label and date it.

Store lavender-infused vinegar in a cool, dry location or in the refrigerator for up to 3 years. Store lavender-infused oil in a cool, dry location for up to 6 months. You can also store the oil in the refrigerator, but it might be hard to pour until it warms to room temperature.

To give a personal touch to a gift, pour the infused vinegar or oil into an attractive glass bottle and seal it with a cork. Melt candle wax until soft, dip a small paintbrush into the wax, and generously paint the wax around the opening where the cork meets the bottle lip.

While the wax is still warm, push lavender sprigs tied with a jute string into the wax for a farmhouse look. Create a label for the bottle, noting the ingredients, your name as the gift giver, and the date.

Lavender Peach Jam

Serve this luscious jam on hot biscuits, buttered toast, or old-fashioned peanut butter and jelly sandwiches. It also shows up on the Farm Favorite Jammy Pork Loin (page 90). This purist recipe relies on the natural pectin in the fruit and a long cooking process to reduce the mixture to produce a truer fruit flavor. You can purée the peaches before cooking if you prefer a smoother texture, but I like the chunks of peach.

Makes approximately 10 half-pint jars

ingredients

10 cups peeled and diced ripe peaches

9 cups Lavender Sugar (page 76)

½ cup fresh lemon juice

to make

1 Combine the peaches, lavender sugar, and lemon juice in a nonreactive, heavy-bottom pan. Bring to a slow boil over medium or medium-low heat and cook for 15 to 20 minutes, stirring often to prevent scorching.

2 Cook until the mixture is thick and jammy. Test for doneness by dripping some jam onto a chilled plate and tilting the plate to see if the jam runs. If the jam does not set up on the plate, cook for a few minutes longer, testing on another cold plate until it reaches the desired thickness.

3 Pour the jam into sterilized half-pint canning jars. You can process the jam following safe water-bath canning techniques or you can refrigerate the jars and use the jam within 2 months. Alternatively, pour the cooled jam into freezer containers and freeze for up to 1 year.

SAVORY
SURPRISES

*From entrées to sides and meat-forward dishes to vegetarian
fare, these are a few of my favorite savory lavender recipes.*

Sticky Lavender-Honey Chicken

This is my absolute favorite lavender chicken recipe. It's a sweet, lemony, peppery, sticky dish that you will return to again and again. Serve it with a fresh salad and big crusty hunks of French bread to sop up every drop of the delicious lavender cream sauce. It works well with firm tofu, too.

Serves 6

ingredients

- 2 tablespoons Lavender Honey (page 78)
- 4 teaspoons good olive oil, plus more for the pan
- 4 teaspoons fresh lemon juice
- ¼ teaspoon fresh lemon zest
- 1 tablespoon 'Royal Velvet' dried lavender buds, crushed
- ½ teaspoon Lavender Lemon Pepper (page 74), ground, plus more for seasoning
- ⅛ teaspoon, or 2 pinches, Lavender Himalayan Salt (page 72), plus more for seasoning
- 1 cut-up fryer, or 3 pounds chicken fillets
- ¾ cup heavy cream
- ½ teaspoon 'Royal Velvet' dried lavender buds, whole

prepare the chicken

1 Whip together the honey, olive oil, lemon juice, lemon zest, crushed lavender buds, lavender lemon pepper, and lavender salt in a mixing bowl.

2 Add the chicken to the mixing bowl and stir until all the pieces are coated. Cover and marinate the chicken in the refrigerator for a minimum of 30 minutes or up to 24 hours. The best flavor develops if you let it sit for at least 8 hours.

continued on next page

In these recipes, "good" olive oil means extra-virgin olive oil, fresh and cold-pressed. Check brands for a quality seal such as the North American Olive Oil Association, the California Olive Oil Council, or the USDA Quality Monitoring Program. Avoid olive oil in a clear bottle labeled extra light.

Sticky Lavender-Honey Chicken *continued*

cook the chicken

3 Preheat the oven to 400°F (200°C). Coat a roasting pan or Dutch oven with olive oil.

4 Add the chicken and the marinade to the roasting pan, making sure each piece is well coated. Bake uncovered for 40 minutes, turning the pieces every 15 minutes. If necessary, cover the dish to prevent the chicken from drying out. It is done when it reaches an internal temperature of 165°F (74°C).

5 While the chicken bakes, make the cream sauce. Place the cream and whole lavender buds in a heavy saucepan and stir. Heat the cream to about 115°F (46°C), no hotter. Remove from the heat and let the lavender infuse for 10 to 15 minutes. Taste after 10 minutes to see if it has developed a subtle and fragrant profile. If left too long, the lavender will overpower the sweetness you are aiming for. As soon as you are happy with the flavor, strain out the buds. (The sauce can be made up to 24 hours in advance. If not using immediately, cover tightly and refrigerate.)

6 When the chicken is done, turn off the oven and move the chicken to a heatproof dish. Put it back in the oven to keep warm while you deglaze the pan. To deglaze: Put the roasting pan on the stovetop over medium heat. Pour the infused cream into the pan and stir, scraping up all the browned bits and juices from the chicken. Heat until the cream is bubbling.

7 Serve the chicken hot, with cream sauce drizzled over each plate. Grind additional lavender lemon pepper and lavender salt on top for an extra burst of flavor.

Broilers and fryers are young chickens, 6 to 8 weeks old, that typically weigh 2½ to 3½ pounds. Roasters (less than 8 months old) are a bit bigger, up to 5 pounds, while stewers (usually hens older than 10 months) weigh up to 7 pounds.

Savory Surprises

Lavender Pecan Salmon

We have friends who own a large commercial fishing company in Alaska—so you can bet that they know their salmon. After trying this recipe, they swear it is their favorite way to prepare and cook the fish. That's a pretty good endorsement! It just might become your favorite, too.

Serves 4

ingredients

- 2 tablespoons 'Royal Velvet' or 'Provence' dried lavender buds
- ¾ cup raw pecans or hazelnuts, coarsely chopped
- ¼ cup good olive oil
- 2 tablespoons Dijon mustard
- ¼ cup Lavender Honey (page 78)
- ¾ cup fresh basil or lemon balm, chopped
- ⅛ teaspoon, or 2 pinches, Lavender Himalayan Salt (page 72), plus more for seasoning
- 1½–2 pounds salmon fillets, 1–1½-inches thick
- Lavender Lemon Pepper (page 74)
- Lemon wedges for garnish

to make

1. Preheat the oven to 375°F (190°C).

2. Toast the lavender buds in a dry pan over medium heat, stirring constantly until toasty brown; 30 seconds to a minute. Watch carefully so they don't burn.

3. Remove the lavender from the heat and toss with the nuts, olive oil, mustard, lavender honey, basil, and lavender salt.

4. Place the salmon in a lightly oiled baking dish or shallow roasting pan. Season both sides with lavender lemon pepper and additional lavender salt to taste.

5. Heap the lavender-nut mixture on top of the salmon, pressing it into the fillets. Don't worry if some of the mixture spills around the sides; just sprinkle it back on the salmon when serving.

6. Bake for 25 minutes, or until the salmon reaches an internal temperature of 130°F (54°C). Serve immediately with the lemon wedges.

Farm Favorite Jammy Pork Loin

My boys love this flavorful dish served with green beans and buttered mashed potatoes, with the pan glaze from the pork loin drizzled over everything. You can substitute a rolled turkey breast tenderloin for the pork loin.

Serves 4

ingredients

1–2 tablespoons olive or avocado oil

¾ cup Lavender Peach Jam (page 83)

2 tablespoons Dijon mustard

3 tablespoons aged balsamic vinegar

¼ teaspoon 'Provence' dried lavender buds

¼ teaspoon Peppender (page 75)

2 pounds pork loin

Lavender Lemon Pepper (page 74)

Lavender Himalayan Salt (page 72)

Water or white wine, for deglazing

to make

1 Preheat the oven to 375°F (190°C). Oil a cast-iron Dutch oven or other heavy roasting pan.

2 Combine the jam, mustard, vinegar, lavender buds, and Peppender. Mix until well blended. Set aside.

3 Remove the visible fat from the loin, then rinse the meat and pat as dry as possible.

4 Put the loin in the Dutch oven, turning it in the oil to coat both sides. Season on both sides with lavender lemon pepper and lavender salt. Spread ¼ cup of the jam mixture on top of the meat.

5 Cook uncovered for 40 minutes, or until the meat reaches an internal temperature of 145°F (63°C). While the pork is roasting, baste with any jam mixture that melts off the pork to prevent it burning into the bottom of the pan.

6 After 40 minutes, pour the remaining jam mixture over the pork. Cook for an additional 10 minutes. Remove from the oven and let rest for 10 minutes before carving.

7 While the pork is resting, deglaze the roasting pan with ¼ to ½ cup water. Spoon the hot sauce over the sliced pork before serving.

Pine Creek Farm Peposo (Tuscan Stew)

My husband, Rick, was born in Pittsburgh, and he grew up in an Italian family in an Italian neighborhood. He inherited his amazing culinary skills from his mom and dad, who were cooks and bakers extraordinaire. This hands-down favorite beef dish is always on our Christmas table! We serve it over creamy polenta with warm Italian bread to soak up the incredible sauce. *Mangia!*

Don't be tempted to reduce or omit the pepper—it mellows to a rich deep flavor as it becomes infused in the wine.

Serves 6

ingredients

- 3 tablespoons good olive oil
- 6 bone-in beef short ribs (8–10 ounces each)
- Lavender Himalayan Salt (page 72)
- 1 tablespoon tomato paste
- 2 tablespoons Peppender (page 75), finely ground
- 8 cloves garlic, peeled and crushed
- 3 small sage leaves
- 2 bay leaves
- 3 small sprigs 'Provence' dried lavender or rosemary
- 2 cups red wine, preferably Chianti
- 2 tablespoons Lavender Lemon Pepper (page 74), coarsely ground

to make

1. Heat the olive oil over medium-high heat in a large Dutch oven. Season the short ribs with lavender salt and braise each side for a minute or two until well browned. Braise them in batches if necessary to make sure they are thoroughly browned. Set the meat aside on a plate.

2. Add the tomato paste, Peppender, garlic, sage, bay leaves, lavender sprigs, and wine to the meat juices in the Dutch oven. Stir, then return the meat to the pan.

3. Cover and simmer over low heat for 1½ hours.

4. Uncover and add the lavender lemon pepper.

5. Cover again and simmer for another 1½ to 2 hours, turning the meat occasionally, until the wine has been absorbed and the sauce has reduced. The short ribs should be fork-tender but not completely falling apart.

Provence Farm-Style Tomato Soup

Visitors call our farm "Provence in Pine" (Pine, Arizona, that is!) all the time. Perhaps it's the historic farmhouse at the top of the hill. Perhaps it's the beautiful fields of lavender surrounded by green trees. Whatever the reason, I think this simple but amazing soup, served with oven-hot Lavender and Olive Focaccia Bread (page 118), is good enough to stand up with any that's made in France.

Serves 6

ingredients

- 1 rounded tablespoon Lavender Herbes de Provence (page 73)
- 2 (10½-ounce) cans of your favorite condensed tomato soup, water added per the directions (or 1 quart prepared tomato soup)
- 2 (16-ounce) cans diced tomatoes
- Good olive oil for drizzling

to make

1 Make a bouquet garni by placing the herbes de Provence in a disposable loose-leaf tea bag and closing it tightly.

2 Add the soup, diced tomatoes, and bouquet garni to a large pot. Warm over medium-low heat to infuse the soup with the herbs, stirring and tasting often until you love the flavor profile. (We let the herbs infuse for about 15 minutes.)

3 Remove the herbs, then heat the soup over high heat to just boiling.

4 Serve immediately with a drizzle of olive oil.

Use a brand of diced tomatoes that doesn't contain calcium chloride or other firming agents. They make the tomatoes too firm.

Vegetarian Curry

If you love lavender, you will love this easy vegetarian recipe. Its flavors evoke exotic gastronomic adventures, but really, it's a down-home farm stew. Serve it over rice with warm lavender salted naan (naan bread brushed with butter and lots of freshly ground lavender salt, then run under a broiler until golden brown).

Serves 4

ingredients

- 4 tablespoons good olive oil
- 1 teaspoon 'Provence' dried lavender buds
- 1 clove garlic
- 1 teaspoon Peppender (page 75), plus more for seasoning
- 1–4 hot chiles or peppers, such as Thai chile, serrano pepper, jalapeño, or habanero pepper (select based on your heat tolerance)
- 1 small butternut squash or large acorn squash, peeled and cubed
- 1 red bell pepper, diced
- 1 (19-ounce) can chickpeas, drained, or 1½ cups home-cooked
- 1 rounded teaspoon grated fresh ginger (optional)
- 1 (13½-ounce) can coconut cream
- Lavender Himalayan Salt (page 72)
- ¼ cup water
- 2 limes, cut into wedges, for garnish (optional)
- 4 tablespoons fresh cilantro, chopped, for garnish (optional)
- 2 tablespoons fresh Thai basil, chopped, for garnish (optional)

to make

1 Heat the olive oil in a large pan over medium-high heat. Add the lavender buds, garlic, Peppender, and chiles, and cook until just browned.

2 Add the squash, bell pepper, and chickpeas to the hot oil and cook until sizzling.

3 Immediately stir in the ginger, if using, and coconut cream; add lavender salt and more Peppender to taste.

4 Cook over medium heat until the squash is tender, about 20 minutes. If the curry is too dry, add up to ¼ cup water to achieve the desired consistency.

5 Remove from the heat and serve piping hot, garnished with lime wedges, cilantro, and Thai basil, if using.

Watermelon Summer Salad

When salad starts showing up on the farm table, lavender harvest is not far off. This dish is perfect when watermelon is at its peak flavor. Fresh lettuce and sweet watermelon dressed with crunchy lavender roasted nuts and creamy cheese couldn't be more harmonious. It's deceptively simple, but always gets rave reviews!

Serves 4

ingredients

- 1 cup raw pecans or walnuts
- ¼ cup Lavender Sugar (page 76) or Lavender Honey (page 78)
- 2 tablespoons warm water
- ¼ cup Lavender Honey
- ¼ cup apple cider vinegar or white balsamic vinegar
- ⅛ cup good olive oil
- 2 teaspoons Peppender (page 75)
- 2 cups watermelon cubes
- ¼ teaspoon Lavender Himalayan Salt (page 72)
- 1 large head romaine or Bibb lettuce
- 1 (8-ounce) round of goat cheese or 8 ounces fresh mozzarella, cubed

to make

1 Put the nuts in a dry skillet over medium heat and toast lightly, stirring constantly for a few minutes. When the nuts are just barely toasted, add the lavender sugar. Reduce the heat and continue to stir until the sugar melts and coats the nuts. Transfer the nuts to a plate to cool.

2 Pour the warm water and lavender honey into a half-pint canning jar and stir to dissolve. Add the vinegar, olive oil, and Peppender. Top with a lid and shake thoroughly. (You can double or triple this recipe for convenience. It keeps, refrigerated, for up to 4 weeks.)

3 Put the watermelon in a large bowl. Sprinkle the lavender salt over the watermelon and toss to combine.

4 Tear the lettuce into bite-size pieces and add to the bowl. Add the cheese and the dressing and toss to combine.

5 Top with the roasted nuts just before serving.

Lavender Roasted Potatoes

These creamy, crispy potatoes will become your go-to side dish! Match it with any dinner entrée, pair with a crisp salad for lunch, or use as a showstopping addition to breakfast.

Serves 4–6

ingredients

- 8 medium thin-skinned potatoes such as red potatoes or Yukon Gold potatoes

  Good olive oil

- 2 teaspoons 'Provence' dried lavender buds, finely chopped

- ½ teaspoon Lavender Himalayan Salt (page 72)

- ½ teaspoon Lavender Lemon Pepper (page 74)

- 1 tablespoon garlic, minced (optional)

  Italian parsley for garnish (optional)

to make

1 Preheat the oven to 400°F (200°C).

2 Chop the potatoes into halves or thirds and place in a shallow roasting pan or sheet pan. Drizzle them liberally with olive oil and sprinkle with the lavender buds, lavender salt, lavender lemon pepper, and garlic, if using. Toss well.

3 Bake the potatoes for 30 minutes.

4 Plate individually or family-style on a platter and sprinkle with parsley, if using, for garnish.

This is a great recipe for a vegetable blend—think summer squash, green beans, cherry tomatoes, and bell peppers. Add a tablespoon of lavender honey to the olive oil and stir well before drizzling over the vegetables and adding the rest of the seasoning. It's also great on Brussels sprouts!

BAKING WITH LAVENDER

It doesn't get much better than a lavender chocolate cake. Except for maybe a lavender lemon Italian morning cake. Or lavender cinnamon rolls! If you can't tell, I love sweets, and I think you'll also love these lavender sweet treats.

Lavender Chocolate Cake

When members of the Arizona Office of Tourism visited our farm, I made a Lavender Chocolate Cake to mark the occasion. In the excitement, I discovered at the last minute that I had no confectioners' sugar to make the frosting. Then I realized that our superfine Pine Creek Farm Lavender Cocoa would be a great substitute. And indeed, it made the most delicious, cloudlike frosting! Expect rave reviews and pleas for the recipe.

Serves 12–15 (city servings, that is; here at the farm, it's more like 8–10!)

for the cake

½ cup grapeseed oil

1 cup milk

2 eggs

1 cup granulated sugar

1 cup Lavender Sugar (page 76)

1 teaspoon instant coffee granules

1½ teaspoons baking soda

1½ teaspoons baking powder

1 teaspoon Lavender Himalayan Salt (page 72)

¾ cup extra-dark unsweetened cocoa powder

1¾ cups all-purpose flour

1 cup water, brought to a boil

for the frosting

½ cup (1 stick) butter, softened

1 (5-ounce) tin Pine Creek Farm Lavender Cocoa or ¼ cup Dutch process cocoa + 2 tablespoons finely ground confectionary lavender

3 tablespoons heavy cream

Lavender sugar and sprigs of lavender for garnish

to make

1 Preheat the oven to 350°F (180°C). Grease and flour two 9-inch cake pans.

2 Combine the grapeseed oil, milk, and eggs in the bowl of a stand mixer or by hand in a large bowl.

3 Stir in the granulated sugar and lavender sugar. Add the coffee, baking soda, baking powder, lavender salt, and cocoa. Blend thoroughly. Add the flour and stir to combine.

4 Add the boiling water and stir to make a thin batter.

continued on next page

5   Pour the batter into the prepared cake pans. Bake for 30 to 35 minutes. Remove from oven and cool thoroughly before frosting.

6   To make the frosting, cream the butter and cocoa in a medium bowl with a hand mixer. Add the cream as needed until the mixture is light and fluffy, about 5 minutes.

7   Frost the cake and decorate with lavender sugar and/or sprigs of lavender, if desired.

Powdered lavender was used as a food preservative and flavoring in medieval times.

Lemon-Lavender Sandwich Cookies

This is hands down one of the best cookies in the known universe. It offers an ideal balance of lavender and lemon and is crispy on the outside, chewy on the inside. Plus, it's just as beautiful to admire as it is delicious to eat. This recipe makes a generous amount of frosting. If you have any left over, pull out the graham crackers!

Makes 12–16 sandwich cookies

for the cookies

2½ cups all-purpose flour

½ teaspoon salt

½ teaspoon baking powder

¼ teaspoon baking soda

1 cup (2 sticks) butter

2 cups Lavender Sugar (page 76), plus more for rolling

2 eggs

2 tablespoons lemon zest

2 tablespoons fresh lemon juice

for the frosting

2 cups Lavender Sugar

½ cup (1 stick) butter, softened

2 tablespoons fresh lemon juice

3 drops AmeriColor Soft Gel Paste food coloring: 469 Lilac

Lavender buds for garnish

to make

1 Preheat the oven to 350°F (180°C). Line two cookie sheets with parchment paper.

2 Combine the flour, salt, baking powder, and baking soda in a medium bowl. Set aside.

3 Cream the butter and lavender sugar until light and fluffy in the bowl of a stand mixer or by hand in a large bowl. Add the eggs, lemon zest, and lemon juice. Beat until well combined.

4 Add the flour mixture and stir until combined. Be careful not to overmix.

5 Form the dough into walnut-size balls. Roll each ball in lavender sugar. Place the balls 3 inches apart on the prepared cookie sheets.

6 Bake for 12 minutes, or until lightly browned and cracked on top. Remove from the cookie sheets and allow to cool completely before frosting.

continued on next page

7   Meanwhile, make the frosting. Combine the lavender sugar, butter, and lemon juice in a medium bowl. Whip until firm. Add the food coloring for a subtle lavender hue.

8   To assemble the cookies, spread a heaping tablespoon of frosting on the bottom of one cookie, then sandwich another cookie on top. Decorate with a dab of frosting and lavender buds.

Instead of food coloring, I often whip 1 heaping tablespoon of fresh blueberries in the frosting for a natural, lovely tint. I love experimenting with natural colors and have used beet root powder and pea flower powder to achieve a lavender color in foods without adding artificial ingredients.

Lavender Cinnamon Rolls

This recipe delivers incredible cinnamon rolls thanks to our secret step: prepping the baking dish with lots of butter, lots of cream, and lots of sugar. It may not be the healthiest, but I promise you that this combination is pure lavender heaven.

These cinnamon rolls are perfect on a chilly winter morning. As soon as they smell the sweet scent wafting through the house, your family will come running to the kitchen table.

Makes 12 rolls

for the dough

- 1 tablespoon Lavender Honey (page 78) (if you don't have lavender honey, sub lavender sugar)
- ¼ cup warm water
- 1 package active dry yeast
- ½ cup warm milk
- ½ teaspoon salt
- 1 egg
- ½ cup (1 stick) butter, softened
- ¼ cup Lavender Sugar (page 76)
- 3 cups (approximate) all-purpose flour

for the filling

- 1 cup raw pecans or walnuts
- ½ cup Lavender Sugar
- ½ cup (1 stick) butter, softened
- 1 cup firmly packed dark brown sugar
- 2 tablespoons ground cinnamon
- ½ cup raisins (optional)

for the baking dish

- 4 tablespoons butter, melted
- 1 cup heavy cream
- ½ cup firmly packed dark brown sugar
- 1 tablespoon Lavender Sugar
- 1 tablespoon ground cinnamon

for the glaze

- 4 tablespoons butter, softened
- 1½ cups Lavender Sugar
- 3–4 tablespoons milk or lemon juice

continued on next page

Lavender Cinnamon Rolls *continued*

make the dough

1 Warm a small bowl. Add to it the lavender honey and warm water, stir, then sprinkle the yeast on top. Let sit until the yeast dissolves and bubbles begin to form, about 2 minutes.

2 Warm the bowl of a stand mixer, or a large bowl if working by hand, then add the yeast mixture, milk, salt, egg, butter, and lavender sugar. Mix on medium speed until well combined, then add the flour 1 cup at a time, mixing well until a soft dough is formed.

3 Remove the dough from the mixer and place in a large, oiled bowl. Turn the dough once to oil all sides. Cover with plastic wrap, set aside in a warm area, and let sit for 60 minutes or until the dough has doubled in size.

toast the nuts

4 While the dough is rising, toast the nuts in a dry pan over medium heat, stirring occasionally until just beginning to brown. Then sprinkle ¼ cup of the lavender sugar over them and stir constantly until the sugar melts and coats the nuts.

5 Immediately remove the nuts from the heat and spread on parchment paper or a sheet pan to cool.

assemble the cinnamon rolls

6 Remove the plastic wrap and punch down the dough. Transfer the dough to a floured surface. Roll the dough into a 9- × 15-inch rectangle, ½ to ¾ inch thick.

7 Create the filling by spreading the butter evenly over the dough, then distribute the toasted nuts, the remaining ¼ cup lavender sugar, brown sugar, cinnamon, and raisins (if using) evenly and all the way to the edges of the dough.

8 Starting on the long side of the rectangle, roll the dough over the filling to form a log. Roll evenly and firmly without compressing the dough. End with the seam side down.

final rise & bake

9 Prepare the baking dish: Pour the melted butter over the bottom of a 9- × 12-inch baking dish. Pour in the cream. Distribute the brown sugar, lavender sugar, and cinnamon over the butter and cream.

10 Cut the cinnamon roll log into 12 slices, each about 1½ inches thick. Place the slices side by side into the prepared baking dish, fitting all 12 into the dish. It's fine if you have to squeeze them tightly next to one another. Set aside, covered or uncovered, in a warm place for 30 minutes to let the dough rise again.

11 Preheat the oven to 350°F (180°C).

12 Place the baking dish on the middle rack and bake for 20 to 25 minutes, until the rolls are just golden brown.

make the glaze

13 Whip together the butter, lavender sugar, and milk into a loose frosting texture. (Substitute lemon juice for the milk for a wonderful lavender-lemon flavor.)

14 While the cinnamon rolls are still warm, spread the glaze evenly over the tops, allowing the glaze to melt into the rolls. Serve immediately.

a note about storage

Both the baked-and-glazed rolls and the unbaked dough freeze well, so it's worth making extra batches.

BAKED AND GLAZED ROLLS.
To freeze a pan of baked cinnamon rolls, tightly cover the pan of rolls in plastic wrap, excluding as much air as possible, then place in a freezer bag or overwrap with foil. Use within 4 months. To serve, remove the wrap or foil, defrost completely at room temperature, then heat at 250°F (120°C) for a few minutes before serving. Add extra glaze if desired.

UNRISEN DOUGH. After step 10, cover the pan of rolls in plastic wrap, excluding as much air as possible, then place in a freezer bag or overwrap with foil. To serve, remove the wrap or foil, then defrost completely at room temperature for 4 to 6 hours or until the rolls have risen, doubling in size. Continue from step 11 to bake and glaze the rolls.

Yeast is a living organism, so when working with yeast dough, keep all ingredients and utensils warm since cold keeps the yeast from growing.

Lavender Lemon Italian Morning Cake

This old Italian family recipe is popular because you only need a pan, a bowl, and a tablespoon to make it. But don't let the simplicity fool you. This cake is as good as any lemon cake you have ever eaten—made all the better with lavender. In fact, it's my family's favorite nonchocolate dessert. It's best served just out of the oven.

Makes one 8-inch cake (single layer, small Bundt, or loaf); for a larger cake, double the recipe.

for the cake

- 2 large eggs
- ½ cup + 2 tablespoons Lavender Sugar (page 76)
- Zest of 2 lemons
- 3 tablespoons fresh lemon juice
- ½ cup + 2 tablespoons milk (nondairy is fine)
- ½ cup + 2 tablespoons grapeseed oil
- ¾ cup all-purpose flour
- 1 teaspoon baking powder

for the glaze

- ¼ cup Lavender Sugar
- 2½ tablespoons fresh lemon juice
- 1 tablespoon lemon zest

to make

1 Preheat the oven to 350°F (180°C). Lightly butter and flour the cake pan.

2 Beat the eggs and lavender sugar until light and fluffy, 4 to 5 minutes. Add the lemon zest, lemon juice, milk, and grapeseed oil, and mix thoroughly. Add the flour and baking powder; continue to beat until smooth. Pour into the prepared pan.

3 Bake for 40 minutes, or until a cake tester comes out clean.

4 While the cake is baking, make the glaze: Mix the lavender sugar with the lemon juice in a pan over medium heat, warming the mixture and stirring until the sugar dissolves completely. Remove from the heat and stir in the lemon zest.

5 Remove the cake from the oven and let cool in the pan for 5 minutes before transferring to a plate. While the cake is still warm, pour the glaze slowly and evenly over the cake.

Fall Spice Lavender-Pumpkin Bread

This moist bread is yummy with a mug of hot coffee on a cool, crisp autumn morning. But it's also great when company comes over. Serve it to your guests warm from the oven with a big dollop of lavender whipped cream.

Makes 2 loaves

for the bread

- 3¼ cups all-purpose flour
- 2 tablespoons ground cinnamon
- 1 tablespoon baking powder
- ½ teaspoon baking soda
- ½ teaspoon freshly ground nutmeg
- ¾ teaspoon Lavender Himalayan Salt (page 72)
- 1 (15-ounce) can pumpkin, or 2 cups fresh pumpkin, cooked and mashed
- 1¾ cups Lavender Sugar (page 76)
- ½ cup firmly packed dark brown sugar
- 4 eggs
- ¾ cup (1½ sticks) butter, melted
- ½ cup milk

for the topping

- ¾ cup heavy cream, chilled
- 2 tablespoons Lavender Sugar

to make

1. Preheat the oven to 350°F (180°C). Butter two loaf pans.

2. Stir the flour, 1 tablespoon of the cinnamon, the baking powder, baking soda, nutmeg, and lavender salt in a bowl. Set aside.

3. Cream the pumpkin, 1½ cups of the lavender sugar, and the brown sugar in the bowl of a stand mixer or by hand in a large bowl, mixing well until light and slightly fluffy. Beat in the eggs one at a time, then add the butter. Mix well.

4. Add about half of the flour mixture, followed by half of the milk. Mix, then add the rest. Divide the batter between the pans.

5. Combine the remaining ¼ cup lavender sugar and remaining 1 tablespoon cinnamon in a small bowl. Sift the mixture over each loaf.

6. Bake the loaves for 60 minutes, or until cake testers come out clean. Remove from the oven and let cool.

7   Make the topping: Using a clean, cold mixing bowl, combine the cream and lavender sugar with a stand mixer and whip until soft peaks form.

8   Thickly slice the bread and serve each slice with a hearty dollop of lavender whipped cream.

This lavender ice cream
tastes just fine on its own,
but I especially like it
topped with a berry sauce.
Or use your imagination
and add chocolate, nuts,
ginger—whatever
you fancy!

Lavender Ice Cream

Get ready to be the hit of your summer parties! I love this recipe because it requires no preheating or cooking. It's my go-to ice cream. It's best when served fresh: Because it doesn't have any commercial emulsifiers, the leftovers end up freezing very hard.

Makes ½ gallon

ingredients

- 1 quart heavy cream
- 1 quart half-and-half or whole milk
- 1 teaspoon vanilla extract
- 1½ cups Lavender Sugar (page 76)
- 4 tablespoons crushed, freeze-dried blueberries or 3–6 drops Americolor Soft Gel Paste food color: 469 Lilac, for color (optional)

to make

Combine the heavy cream, half-and-half, vanilla, lavender sugar, and coloring, if using, in an ice cream maker and freeze according to the manufacturer's instructions.

If you don't have an ice cream maker, combine all ingredients in a large bowl. Pour into a shallow freezer-safe dish and freeze for 30 minutes. Remove and stir. Repeat the process until the desired consistency is reached.

Lavender and Olive Focaccia Bread

Fresh culinary lavender flowers and leaves really shine in this simple, Mediterranean focaccia, but dried lavender works beautifully, too. Pair with Provence Farm-Style Tomato Soup (page 94). This bread is also tasty with a dipping bowl of olive oil and lavender balsamic vinegar.

Makes 1 loaf

ingredients

3 cups self-rising flour, sifted

12 ounces beer, any kind

3 tablespoons Lavender Sugar (page 76)

2 tablespoons fresh lavender buds and leaves, minced; or 2 tablespoons dried lavender buds

4 tablespoons butter, softened

¼ cup pitted kalamata olives

Lavender Himalayan Salt (page 72)

Lavender Lemon Pepper (page 74)

to make

1   Preheat the oven to 375°F (190°C). Cover a baking sheet with parchment paper or sprinkle cornmeal on a baking stone. For a crispier crust, preheat the baking stone before sprinkling on the cornmeal.

2   Mix the flour, beer, lavender sugar, lavender buds and leaves, and butter in the bowl of a stand mixer, or by hand in a large bowl, until well combined.

3   Turn the dough onto a floured work surface and knead six times. Form into a round loaf.

4   Place the loaf on the baking sheet or stone. Press the olives evenly into the loaf, taking care not to collapse the dough. Liberally grind lavender salt and lavender lemon pepper over the top.

5   Bake for 60 minutes, or until lightly browned.

6   Serve hot and crusty, right out of the oven.

LAVENDER MIXOLOGY

*Lavender isn't just for roasting, marinating, sautéing, and baking.
It also makes a delightful addition to your favorite drink,
whether it's a boozy margarita or a refreshing glass of iced tea.
It's simple: Lavender is relaxing and alcohol is relaxing,
so it's no wonder lavender cocktails are a perfect pairing!*

All-Natural Lavender Margarita

Imagine pairing the soothing scent of a lavender field with the *olé!* of tequila. Then let me introduce you to our lavender margarita. It marries Lavender Simple Syrup and fresh citrus for a fragrant and refreshing drink.

Makes 2 drinks

ingredients

- 4 ounces Lavender Simple Syrup (page 77)
- 4 ounces fresh lime or lemon juice; use the rind for twists
- 6–8 ounces of your favorite tequila
- Ice
- Lavender Himalayan Salt (page 72) or Lavender Sugar (page 76) to rim the glasses
- 2 lavender sprigs for garnish

to make

Stir the lavender simple syrup, lime juice, and tequila in a shaker or small pitcher. Wet the rims of two glasses with the citrus rind and coat with lavender salt. Let dry, then fill the glasses with ice. Divide the margarita between the glasses and garnish each with a lavender sprig and a twist.

Instead of the traditional salted rim, make a bold lavender statement by heavily coating just one side of the glass with salt. To do this, twirl the glass in lime juice along one side, focusing on the outside of the glass, then dip that side in lavender salt.

Lavender Alligator

Mint, lime, and lavender is a combination that's truly too good to be true. So simple to make, but beware: This cocktail is strong!

Makes 4 drinks

ingredients

- 1 (12-ounce) can frozen limeade
- 12 ounces vodka or white rum
- 1 cup fresh mint leaves, tightly packed
- 3 tablespoons culinary lavender, fresh or dried buds
- Ice
- 4 lavender sprigs for garnish

to make

1 Place the limeade, vodka, mint, and lavender buds in a blender, then add as much ice as will fit.

2 Blend into a smooth slush.

3 Pour the mixture into chilled glasses and garnish each glass with a lavender sprig.

Lavender Lattes and Cocoas

Farm life keeps us busy, so we don't often have time to pop into a coffeehouse for a gourmet coffee or cocoa. That's why we love these hot lavender drinks that can be made at home in a few minutes.

latte

⅔ cup hot coffee

½ cup whole milk, warmed

2 tablespoons Lavender Simple Syrup (page 77)

Pour the ingredients into a mug and take a little break!

cocoa

1½ tablespoons unsweetened cocoa powder

1 cup whole milk

3 tablespoons Lavender Simple Syrup

Heat the ingredients in a pan, stirring to dissolve the cocoa. Pour into a mug and relax for a while!

Lavender Mint Sun Tea

This is such a refreshing summer drink, but you can make it all winter long or on cloudy days. If the sun's not out, use boiling water instead of cold. (Just be sure your jar is safe for high temperatures; canning jars work well.) Steep for 10 to 15 minutes, then add Lavender Sugar or Lavender Honey, if desired.

If you don't have access to fresh lavender and fresh mint, use 1½ tablespoons dried lavender buds and 3 tablespoons dried mint leaves. Put them in a disposable loose-leaf tea bag or tie them up in a square of cheesecloth before adding to the jar.

Makes 1 quart

ingredients

3 stalks fresh 'Royal Velvet' or 'Provence' lavender

½ cup fresh mint leaves, tightly packed

1 quart cold water

½ cup Lavender Sugar (page 76) or Lavender Honey (page 78) (optional)

to make

1 Muddle the lavender and mint in the bottom of a quart jar. Add the water. For sweet tea, add the lavender sugar and stir thoroughly to dissolve.

2 Seal the jar and set it in direct sunlight, preferably outside, to infuse for several hours. Shake the jar occasionally.

3 Serve the tea over ice.

4
planting, harvesting, and drying
LAVENDER

A perennial, drought-tolerant herb that can live for 15 years or more, lavender is an extremely adaptive wonder. It can be a successful houseplant, works beautifully in containers on patios, and makes a fragrant addition to nearly any garden. If you have the notion, you can plant fields of it and grow a full-fledged crop! The secret is to pick varieties that suit your purpose. We discuss several lavender varieties in Chapter 1 to help you get an idea of the diversity of lavender.

To cultivate your own lavender, keep these two important things in mind: Lavender needs plenty of sun and plenty of drainage. This chapter offers tips on growing lavender based on our experience here at Pine Creek Lavender Farm, but there are many encyclopedic gardening resources that walk you through the process in more detail. If you're interested in expanding your garden or home landscape with lavender, see page 155 for some references.

Choosing a Cultivar

Lavender is generally easy to grow as long as you pay attention to its likes and dislikes and plant the right varieties for your area. English lavender varieties are often recommended for cool or temperate conditions, while Spanish varieties are recommended for hot climates. Keep in mind that microclimates and automated watering systems can create humidity and deliver too much water—conditions that can kill your lavender plants, no matter where you live. If you recognize that lavender has different needs from your typical garden plants and give it what it needs, it's a wonderfully forgiving plant!

How Will You Use It?

Before you choose specific types of lavender, there are a couple of things to think about.

First, consider how you plan to use lavender. Is it mainly for decorative purposes in your garden or landscape plan? Will you want to harvest it to use fresh or dried? We often recommend the following for gardens.

'GROSSO'—great for hedges and tall plantings; has beautiful dark blue and purple flowers with good drying properties for crafts and oil

MANY ENGLISH VARIETIES—best for cold-weather tolerance; beautiful, if shorter flowers; easy success for newbie growers

SPANISH LAVENDER VARIETIES—high heat and drought tolerance; distinctive flower shape; comes in purple, pink, and white; not recommended for culinary purposes and is considered toxic to animals

Second, do you want to use your lavender for culinary purposes in cooking, baking, and mixology recipes? If so, we recommend planting most English varieties, as well as 'Provence'. We like 'Provence' for its peppery flavor (great in savory dishes) and English varieties like 'Royal Velvet' (which has a sweet, mild flavor profile) for confectionary uses and to sweeten a spirit-forward cocktail.

Be sure to source your plants from a reputable nursery to ensure they are, in fact, culinary varieties.

The Right Lavender for Your Region

Though its origins trace back to the Mediterranean and Middle East, where wild lavender still grows, lavender is now cultivated in a variety of climates. Areas for growing lavender successfully have moderate year-round temperatures and bright, sunny summers. We know lavender growers across the nation and have learned how big snows and late hard freezes can cause problems for them. For example, friends in Pennsylvania lost hundreds of plants one year in a huge snowfall.

The first step to growing your own lavender is to determine your U.S. Department of Agriculture (USDA) growing zone. The USDA's Plant

Hardiness Zone Map is the gold standard by which gardeners and growers determine the plants that are most likely to thrive in any region. The map is divided into 11 zones based on the average annual minimum winter temperature.

To locate your zone, visit the USDA zone map website and enter your zip code in the search box. Pine, Arizona, is in Zone 7a, which we have found to be perfect for growing both the true lavenders (*L. angustifolia*) such as 'Royal Velvet' as well as *Lavandula* × *intermedia* varieties, like 'Grosso' and 'Provence'.

For local customers who want to grow lavender for landscapes and gardens, we suggest planting the lavender on the north side of the house or in containers that can be moved when the summer sun is most intense.

For regions that get a lot of rain, make sure the lavender plants have excellent soil drainage to help avoid root rot.

For regions colder than Zone 5, grow lavender in containers that can live indoors during winter.

The Victorians planted lavender as hedges and in gardens, and both Queen Victoria and Queen Elizabeth are said to have used lavender products from Yardley of London, a fragrance and cosmetics firm established in 1770.

Lavender that begins to droop needs a drink! Some farmers like to dig down a foot into the soil to see if they can form a ball of soil. If so, it's still moist enough for the lavender plants.

Soil and Water Requirements

Most experienced gardeners assume that rich soil, a moisture-retaining layer of mulch or compost, and consistent moisture will lead to a healthy plant. Not so with lavender! This plant prefers poor, dry, slightly alkaline soil, and it hates having wet feet. Plant the herb in sandy soil, ideally with a pH of 7.0, and make sure the water drains thoroughly from the site. At our farm, the elk do the fertilizing for us, so we don't add fertilizer after our initial application using a well-balanced pH with low acid and burn.

Although lavender is a drought-tolerant plant, that doesn't mean we don't water our fields. The climate here is dry and warm during summer until our seasonal monsoon rains start—usually from early July through September. Therefore, we water more frequently than our fellow lavender farmers in Washington and Oregon, the South, and the Northeast. We water each plant with approximately one gallon of water once a week throughout the growing season, increasing to twice a week a few weeks before harvest, or during hot and dry conditions.

Once we are getting frequent afternoon rains, we generally stop watering the fields unless it gets really hot. Lavender that begins to droop needs a drink! Some farmers like to dig down a foot into the soil to see if they can form a ball of soil. If so, it's still moist enough for the lavender plants!

Lavender and pH

The pH scale shows a soil's alkalinity or acidity level. Soils that are acidic measure 0 to 6 on the pH scale and soils that are alkaline measure 8 to 15. Soil pH measures how many hydrogen ions are affecting the plant roots. The more ions in the soil, the more acidic it will be.

First, it's important to know that lavender favors alkaline conditions. You can have your soil tested at a lab or test it yourself with an inexpensive kit or a soil meter found at home and garden centers. A basic soil-testing kit is accurate for pH levels, calcium, and other minerals.

Hoses run between the rows of lavender plants. Note the relatively weed-free soil between the rows.

Transplanting Lavender

Plant lavender in spring after your average last frost date. We plant from late April through May, which gives the lavender starts a good month to become established before hotter weather rolls in.

1 For nursery-bought plants or divisions of existing plants as we're doing here, dig holes the same depth as the original container or plant division but slightly wider. It's important not to plant young plants too deeply. When we plant baby lavender plants, we mix in one tablespoon of a well-balanced pH and low acid and burn fertilizer to each planting hole. Clipping off the buds will encourage the plant to focus its energy on root growth in the first year.

2 Make sure the soil is just to the level where the crown meets the stem.

3 Don't mulch around the plants, as lavender doesn't like being smothered. Water new plants well for the first weeks while the roots are becoming established. After that, water when the top two inches of soil are dry. Further fertilizing of mature plants isn't necessary.

Elk tracks
between
the rows

Why No Mulch?

There are two reasons growers don't mulch lavender with traditional mulch and compost.
First, unlike many plants, lavender likes alkaline conditions. Most commercial mulch is acidic
and therefore breaks down into the soil, adding undesirable levels of acid to the growing
environment.

Second, traditional mulches and compost tend to accumulate and build up soil levels,
retaining moisture around the base of the plant. For lavender, this is a sure route to poor
plant production and ultimately will kill the plants, as excess moisture often leads to mold,
bacteria, and fungus that will rot lavender roots. Some growers use gravel, weed cloth, or
closely mown grass or other cover crops with a low profile that generally do not accumulate
moisture or introduce acid elements to the growing environment.

There is a lot of disagreement about the use of moisture-retaining plastic and other weed
prevention cloth among growers, so the DIY lavender gardener can choose whether to mulch
with one of these alternatives. At Pine Creek Lavender Farm, we do not mulch or use weed
cloth. We think our lavender breathes a sigh of relief after a yearly raking—usually done in
early spring—to remove all the windblown winter debris from around the plants. Then we
hose off the base of each plant to further remove dried plant matter while giving it a good
soaking to start the year off.

Planting, Harvesting, and Drying Lavender

Blooming Season

Lavender stems can grow from as short as 3 inches to as tall as 18 inches, depending on the variety. The longer the stem, the better for clipping and using in fresh floral bouquets.

Lavender has a main bloom in spring or summer and, depending on the variety, may have a second bloom in fall. The length of the season depends on the climate; in regions with warmer temperatures, the season lasts longer and offers more opportunities for lavender's bloom cycles, or frequencies. There are three types of bloom frequencies:

ONCE—plants may have a smaller, second bloom if flowers are cut early enough.

TWICE—plants produce a full second bloom after the first harvest.

CONTINUOUSLY—plants produce blooms all season long.

'FOLGATE'
Early-blooming lavenders include 'Bowles Early', 'Folgate', and 'Tucker's Early'.

'MADRID PURPLE'
All-season bloomers include 'Buena Vista', 'Croxton's Wild', and 'Madrid Purple'.

Planting, Harvesting, and Drying Lavender

As a small family operation, we can employ sustainable practices at every stage of production, so we do all our harvesting by hand to protect pollinators.

Pruning Lavender

We prune our plants as we harvest, which for us is in early July, cutting off damaged stems as we go. Home growers can prune in fall to prevent the lavender from getting straggly or woody.

Trim each plant back to a mounded shape, cutting back to within 3 inches of the woody part of the plant.

A full-grown lavender bush can produce 6 to 12 bundles (measured by grabbing a handful of stems for cutting) each season.

Harvesting Blooms

Lavender plants do not all produce flowers at the same time on each plant, so we harvest according to where the majority of the plants of any given variety are in their maturing stage. Because we use most of our lavender for culinary products, we want lots of buds for drying. Generally, we are looking for "pop," or flowers just starting to open at the top of the stem. For us, harvesting too soon means that the lavender flower stem has not developed enough buds; harvesting too late means it has developed too many mature flowers and is in full bloom.

Growers who are looking for the highest yield for essential oil, on the other hand, tend to wait until most of the plant is in bloom because the best oil is from the flowers.

A full-grown lavender bush can produce 6 to 12 bundles (measured by grabbing a handful of stems for cutting) each season. As with any harvest, timing is key. The three clues to determining the best harvest date are color, flower pop, and pollinators.

SMALL BUT MIGHTY

The power of lavender lies in its tiny buds. As lavender dries, it encapsulates its essential oil in the dried flower bud. When you squeeze the dried bud, you should get a big hit of the lavender scent, a telltale sign of high-quality lavender.

COLOR. With 'Royal Velvet', we want the plants to develop dark blue-purple blossoms. For 'Provence', we look for a lilac hue. For 'Grosso', it's a dark, rich, navy blue color.

FLOWER POP. Spikes are full of flower buds that are swollen and just about to open, but they haven't quite popped yet.

POLLINATORS. Bees and butterflies gather around, ready to pollinate the plants. When they think it's time, so do we!

Harvesting, Drying, and Storing

There are two methods for harvesting: by hand with sharp scissors or gardening scissors, or mechanically. Lavender attracts pollinators like bees and butterflies and so harvesting by machine, as is often done on large commercial farms, is less than ideal because the equipment sweeps up and often destroys these pollinators. Hand-harvesting protects them. As a small family operation, we can employ sustainable practices at every stage of production, so we do all our harvesting by hand.

Using scissors, cut approximately three inches above the woody part of the plant. This ensures the longest stems of lavender while still being healthy for the plant. This process also trims the plant in a way that encourages a possible second harvest.

Once the plants are harvested, tie the stems in handful-size bundles, fastening each bundle with a rubber band. Unbent paperclips tucked into the rubber bands make convenient hangers.

Hang the bundles upside down to dry. Your drying area must be dark, dry, and well ventilated to dry lavender evenly and preserve the color; humidity can cause the growth of fungus and mold.

Depending on the weather, lavender can take up to three months to dry completely. Check for stems that break easily rather than bend. Store dried bundles as is in a dark, cool, dry environment, or remove the buds and store in sealed containers. Stored properly, lavender can keep for several years.

Cleopatra is said to have seduced both Julius Caesar and Mark Antony with the scent of lavender.

Debudding Stems

1 Roll a bound bundle of lavender between your hands over a wide container. The buds should release easily and fall off. The exception is 'Royal Velvet', which can sometimes hold on a little tighter. Just keep rolling!

2 Store dried lavender buds in food-safe, airtight containers—glass jars work great, as long as the lids have a gasket.

Use Up Those Stems!

Keep those bare stems—they come in handy in lots of unexpected ways!

- Toss them into kindling when starting a fire.

- Use them to smoke meats or as kebab skewers when grilling.

- Incorporate them into crafts, such as chopping them up for use as stuffing for dolls and pet beds, or wrapping them with twine for use as a smudge stick.

- Scatter them around to repel rodents and scorpions.

As a fun note, the OdySea Aquarium in Scottsdale, Arizona, provides its breeding penguins with bundles of our dried lavender to use as nest material. With its antibacterial and antimicrobial properties, the herb not only keeps nests and eggs cleaner, but it makes them smell better, too!

bringing new life to a
PIONEER FARM

My husband, Rick, and I met in California. Between us we have three grown sons, two daughters-in-law, lots of brothers and sisters, and many nieces and nephews. We're so proud of our big, ever-expanding family.

In 2013, we made our way from San Diego to the high-altitude mountains of Pine, Arizona. In 2015, we bought an abandoned farm in town with a cool stream and nearly 10 acres of land that seemed to beg us to return it back to its pioneer roots. So we left corporate life (me from the world of law and politics, Rick from the world of real estate) and dove into the business of planting, weeding, watering, and harvesting lavender plants.

Maintaining and protecting our country's rural heritage matters to Rick and me, as does offering agritourism opportunities to visitors. We opened a Bob's Red Mill–sponsored cooking and baking school, a lavender test kitchen, and a farm retail store, and then we invited the public to tour the grounds, taste our foods, browse our products, and become part of our farm family. Thus, Pine Creek Lavender Farm was born.

The Original Homestead

The town of Pine was settled in 1879 by Mormon pioneers. These pioneers built homesteads throughout the state, especially in the northern regions near the Utah border. Pine sits almost right in the middle of Arizona, in the shadow of the Mogollon Rim, a 200-mile east-to-west ledge that defines the southern lip of the Colorado Plateau. Pine is a verdant valley in the middle of a mountainous region of ponderosa pine trees, babbling creeks, and roaming elk.

Pine is a small town, just shy of 2,500 people. It was even smaller in the early 1880s, when two Mormon pioneers, Alma Moroni Hunt and Rosetta Schmutz Hunt, passed through on their way to Mesa from Salt Lake City, Utah. The couple fell in love with the rugged mountains and picturesque landscape, and decided to stay, acquiring a parcel of land nestled against the slopes.

They farmed corn and raised cattle. And they grew their family, raising 11 children in their cozy home. Built as a simple two-bedroom farmhouse with a small kitchen and tidy living room, it morphed into a structure of

hand-built additions. There were rooms connecting more rooms, indoor spaces spilling onto outdoor porches and gardens.

Alma and Rosetta's eldest son, John, met his future wife, Annie Belle Lazear, in second grade at the historic Strawberry Schoolhouse situated just down the road from the farm. When they married in 1905, the couple received a portion of the original Hunt homestead as a wedding gift.

This generation of the Hunt family continued to expand the farm's structures, adding outbuildings and cabins around the property. In addition to raising cattle, they also planted fruit orchards. The log cabin that currently houses our lavender-drying operation was built in 1890, and the first hand-hewn log for our house was laid around 1910, with rooms added as John and Annie Belle raised their seven children.

Over the years, as family members passed away or moved on, the farm slowly sank into disrepair and was eventually deserted altogether, with the main farmhouse sitting vacant for nearly 50 years.

The Homestead, Reborn

From the time we moved to Pine, Rick and I had loved the farm and its sprawl of buildings, even though it wasn't much to look at. Every time we passed by, we just knew it had potential—we were itching to get our hands on it and restore it.

Not quite knowing what we were getting into, we became the first owners of this farm and homestead—now honored as a National Historic Landmark—outside the Hunt family.

In 2015, we began the restoration of the farmhouse, taking great care to stay as true as we could to John and Annie Belle's vision. We stripped the linoleum down to the original hardwood floors. We preserved the original wainscoting. We even saved the delicate floral wallpaper that hung in the family's daughters' bedroom.

Quickly depleting our savings to restore the homestead, we soon realized we needed some sort of revenue if we were going to continue. We took inventory: We had acreage. We had historic ditch irrigation water rights. We had alkaline soil and a high-altitude climate. Looking around at this lush land, we wondered if we could grow crops here. And if so, what?

An important consideration was that Pine is home to what some believe to be the largest town herd of elk in the United States. Though beautiful

in their regal elegance, these large creatures that roamed down from the mountain each evening worried us. Would they trample whatever we planted? Would they munch on our carefully tended gardens? Rick then asked the all-important question: *What won't elk eat?*

A quick Google search led us to the answer that changed our lives. Lavender! Elk don't eat lavender. Rick and I looked at each other. *Lavender, really?* We knew nothing about the herb except that once, when Rick and I were first dating, he gave me some lavender essential oil.

We jumped in anyway, visiting other lavender farms in the state to learn everything we could about planting, growing, and harvesting. We enlisted the expertise of Paula Bain of the Farm Service Agency of the Federal Rural Development. The homestead's ditch irrigation rights on Pine Creek granted us access to natural spring water, so we figured out how to build an irrigation system. And we then bought 5,500 lavender plants from Red Rock Lavender Farm in Concho, Arizona. We opted for three varieties: 'Royal Velvet', 'Provence', and 'Grosso'.

In May 2016, nearly 30 people—fellow farmers, friends, and family— joined us for two days to set out our first planting. Since then, our lavender crops have flourished, growing bigger and healthier each year, bursting into purple blooms in late spring and early summer.

Pine Creek Lavender Farm Today

Every year, we welcome about 50,000 visitors from all over the United States to experience our lavender fields. They often tell me this is one of the most beautiful lavender farms they've ever seen.

In the Lavender Cooking and Baking School, I use Annie Belle's old kitchen to teach heritage food techniques and culinary lavender classes, and our fresh lavender is used to make lavender products. We make our farm-crafted lavender products ourselves and with other cottage industry partners— we have all things lavender, from lavender health and beauty items to our lavender cooking and baking line.

We love sharing our Pine Creek Lavender Farm recipes with the world. Other people seem to love them as much as we do: A few of our recipes have even taken home Best of Show awards at the Gila County Fair in Arizona.

I love teaching old-fashioned country skills, many of which are lost as each generation moves further away from farm life. Whether I'm teaching my niece how to make lavender bath bombs or a group of students in the Lavender Cooking and Baking School the process of water-bath canning, passing on to our family and our community a piece of the farm life is near and dear to my heart.

See the farm for yourself!

In 2020, Pine Creek Lavender Farm was featured in an episode of Visit Arizona's "Meet the Makers" series. The series showcases chefs, artists, makers, farmers, and more around the state of Arizona, and we were lucky enough to be part of it. A film crew spent two days with us, capturing life on a lavender farm, from cooking in the old kitchen to watching the elk at sunset. The video went on to win an Emmy Award for cinematography. We'd love to share it with you, so if you have a few minutes, you can watch it (and see the real "stars" of the film, our farm animals!) on the Arizona tourism website. It's also on YouTube!

Of course, we'd also love for you to visit us in person. Anytime you're near Pine, Arizona, stop by and say hello.

Pine Creek Lavender Farm
4223 Pine Creek Canyon Road
Pine, Arizona 85544
619-772-6005
pinelavenderfarm.com

Our Local Partners

Here at the farm, we join forces with other local makers in Arizona. We've been lucky enough to share our fresh lavender with brewers, mixologists, and many others who all proudly use our lavender in their products. If you're in Arizona, stop by these spots to check out their Pine Creek Farm lavender-inspired delights.

- Lavender Drop Martini at Old County Inn, Pine

- Lavender Saison at Arizona Wilderness Brewing, statewide locations

- Lavender Latte, Lavender Lemonade, and Lavender Cocoa at Common Grounds Coffee House, Payson

- Lavender Latte at The Early Bird PHX, Phoenix-area food truck

A FEW RESOURCES

As you cultivate your love for this amazing herb, it's likely you'll find yourself wanting to read more about lavender, attend lavender festivals, find restaurants that feature lavender foods, and shop for lavender products.

UNITED STATES LAVENDER GROWERS ASSOCIATION

The USLGA "was formed to support and promote the United States Lavender industry and allows a collective voice for lavender growers and those interested in, or doing business with, lavender in the U.S."

This is a good go-to resource for both current farmers and would-be lavender growers. The association's website offers information on wholesale vendors, suppliers, farms, events, and festivals. They also offer content such as lavender recipes, craft ideas, and tips for backyard gardening with lavender. https://uslavender.org

Books

Berringer Bader, Sarah. 2012. *The Lavender Lover's Handbook.* Portland, Oregon: Timber Press.

McNaughton, Virginia. 2010. *Lavender: The Grower's Guide.* Portland, Oregon: Timber Press.

ACKNOWLEDGMENTS

With love and appreciation to our kids, Aj and Grace, Andy and Olivia, Luke and Aubrey: Where would I be without you guys? I know you will put to good use those lavender harvest cutters you are getting for Christmas!

And to Rick, my man: With your faith in my dream, you shrugged off your handmade Italian loafers and *GQ* style (sometimes a little reluctantly!) to become a lavender farmer. You keep this place looking as good as it does through your tireless work and designing! Thank you forever for being my true love.

Planting these 5,500 lavender plants made magic happen in a way I could never have anticipated! With endless love, I'd like to thank all our lavender-lovers family, or as we like to say around the farm, our "Lovender" family. These are people who showed up to help plant the lavender farm and who amazingly come back every year to help harvest. (Perhaps beckoned now by kegs of freshly brewed lavender beer and our Farm BBQ!)

To the cooks and bakers who tested recipes for this book, a special thank-you!

To the amazing customers and lavender farm store and products team, you are really the heart and soul of Pine Creek Lavender Farm and are the ones who got us where we are today. Saying thanks just isn't enough.

A huge thank-you to my coauthor, Jessica Dunham. This book would never have happened without her. She is the most amazing writing partner one could ever have. That she is the best wordsmith is obvious. But her heart and sweet soul are in every page of this book.

I have so much appreciation for the team at Storey Publishing. Thank you for your enthusiasm right from the start. You brought my dream to life, literally.

In no particular order, but with very particular gratitude, thank you to these friends who have given so much help along the way:

Brian and Cindy Schooley,
Windy Hills Lavender Farm

Deb and Howard Yost;
the "Howard Method"

Joan and Dick Zimmerman

Sisters, Lori Drea and Linda Birnbaum,
and their husbands, Mark and Ed

The best nieces and nephews, Katerinks
(Katie) and Brian Conchuratt, Sophia,
Jax, Rider and Riley Bee

Our hardworking kids, Aj, Grace,
Andy, Olivia, Luke, and Aubrey

Marie Caron

Karen Perkins

Candy Hammond, Mom Margee

Coni and Doug Stover

Helen and Bill Simmons

Shawn and Nancy Burns

Philip and Devla Mahler

Nancy and Bill Hubbs and family

Barbara Huber

Ashley Estes

Brenda Dominguez

Francisco, Rosa, and family

Patrick and Kristen Laughlin

My sister Brita and Mark Treat

Shari and Bill Ahrendt

John and Susan Haddock

Jason Wilson

Jenna Quirico

Diana S. Diehl

Michelle Riachi

Shawn and Heidi Thomas

Laura Nathan

The James Randall family

Our Farm Bureau agent and
grill master, Duane Ridl

And to my best friends,
Linda and Larry Raber

Special thanks to:
Windy Hill Lavender Farm for contributing
dried lavender for photos

Dave and Laurie Owens, a.k.a. "The Garden
Guy," who introduced and launched
Pine Lavender Farm from anonymity to a
huge television audience: thank you!

Bob's Red Mill, sponsor of our
Lavender Baking School

The Arizona Office of Tourism, especially
Debbie Johnson, whose support of rural
Arizona was instrumental in our success

Jack Chapman, Emmy Award–winning
director and cinematographer and owner
of Red Knight Media

Arizona Highways magazine

PHOENIX magazine

Travel + Leisure magazine

And a heartfelt thanks to our Pine Creek
Lavender Farm team: Kathy and Micky
Hunt, Cassie Hute, Chef Val Yeager, and
Kristie Allen

Sabra Sanders, who ran a million miles
assisting with the photo shoot!

Kallie Sue, Pine Creek Pipercub, and
all our horsies

And to our community of unnamed media
friends, customers, and helpers: Thank you
for your love of us and LAVENDER!

INDEX

shades of lavender, 26–27

sinus pressure, 43

skin care, 2–3. *See also* burns
    Bath and Massage Oil, 41
    Beard Oil, 42
    Face Oil, 35
    Face Wash, 34
    lavender hydrosol, 64
    Sugar Scrub, 31
    Wellness Soak, 32–33

sleep aid, viii, 2
    Eye Pillow, 60
    lavender capsules, 35
    lavender pillows, 1
    lavender rollerball, 43
    Lavender Tea, 44

soups and stews
    Pine Creek Farm Peposo (Tuscan Stew), 93
    Provence Farm-Style Tomato Soup, 94–95

Spanish lavender, 10, 12, 69
    growing, 128–29

sprays
    aromatherapy and sanitizing spray, 37
    Spray Cleaner, 66

stems
    debudding stems, 146
    uses for the stems, 147

stomach soother tip, 2

sweeteners
    Lavender Honey, 78–79
    Lavender Simple Syrup, 77
    Lavender Sugar, 76

T

tea
    Lavender Mint Sun Tea, 124
    Lavender Tea, 44–45

terpenes, 2, 12, 19, 37

transplanting lavender, 134–35

U

United States Lavender Growers Association, 5, 155

USDA's Plant Hardiness Zone, 130–31

V

vinegars and oils, 80–81

W

wellness studies, 2